Unshakable
Faith *for*
Shaky Times

Compiled *by* Joyce Williams

Beacon Hill Press of Kansas City
Kansas City, Missouri

Copyright 2002
by Beacon Hill Press of Kansas City

ISBN 083-412-0208

Printed in the
United States of America

Cover Design: Paul Franitza

Library of Congress Cataloging-in-Publication Data

Unshakable faith for shaky times / compiled by Joyce Williams.
　　p. cm.
　ISBN 0-8341-2020-8 (pbk.)
　1. Christian women—Religious life. I. Williams, Joyce, 1944-
　BV4527 .U57 2002
　248.8'43—dc21

2002010374

10 9 8 7 6 5 4 3 2 1

To my special friends who are
going through shaky times.

Find rest, O my soul, in God alone;
my hope comes from him.
He alone is my rock and my salvation;
he is my fortress, I will not be shaken.
Psalm 62:5-6

CONTENTS

FOREWORD

Melting the bad stuff? It's funny how I never thought of the need for that until I was diagnosed with a brain tumor in March 2001. Hearing those words, "brain tumor," from your doctor will get your attention really quickly! The chemotherapy treatments have been a pain—more than one—to say the least. I've spent more time at home in these months than I have in years.

When Joyce called to ask me to consider writing for this project and told me that the focus would be on faith, I didn't have to think but a moment before responding, "Yes, I'd like to participate. There's no way I could have made it through life without faith that God would get me through. Since I'm going through the shakiest time in my life, I'm really having to lean on my unshakable faith in God in order to carry on."

We brainstormed together about ideas, although I must say I try to be careful how I use my brain these days! After I told her about my tumor, Joyce was dismayed and commiserated with me. When I replied that I felt that the treatments were melting the bad stuff, she quickly responded, "I hope they don't melt anything you're going to need!"

So in this shakiest of all times I keep reminding myself that throughout my life the Lord has always melted the bad stuff. Regardless of what happens, I know He'll let me keep the good stuff—the faith that I need to get me through.

—Barbara Johnson

ACKNOWLEDGMENTS

Special appreciation to

My Heavenly Husband for giving me another chance and then the faith to follow His plan.

Gene, my best friend, Prince Charming, chief editor, and greatest encourager. Thanks for having the faith to believe in this project. Without you there would be no book.

Barbara Johnson for stretching her faith in the shakiest time of her life by helping with this book. Thanks for defining the title and for your enormous encouragement.

All the contributors for sharing their faith from their hearts and souls.

Each reader. May your faith remain unshakable.

Remember:

"I am going to do something in your days that you would not believe, even if you were told" (Hab. 1:5).

INTRODUCTION

Warning: You might not want to read this book!

If you're looking for another self-help book, you'll want to lay this one aside. Frankly, I've done the self-help thing, and it didn't work for me. It's so much better when we totally trust our Father's promises and let Him direct our paths through the quicksand of our lives.

Unshakable Faith for Shaky Times has been written to glorify the sustaining presence, grace, and guidance of the Lord. This book is a smorgasbord of candid stories by godly women from around the world who share their walks of faith. Over and over, their stories challenge us to believe in Him with our whole hearts, souls, minds, and beings. Through poems, prose, laughter, tears, transparency, hope, and grace, you'll find absolute reliance on God scrolled across each page. You'll discover the common thread of faith in our Father that sustains us regardless of the distresses, disasters, diseases, and devastations of life.

Although we live in trembling times with troubling days, our Heavenly Father promises to hold us steady. We just have to hold to His Word unswervingly, and He'll provide rock-solid, unshakable faith for shaky times.

LIZ CURTIS HIGGS

NEWS FROM HOME

*T*he envelope looked harmless enough—a handwritten address in a long, looping scrawl, a familiar name in the corner, a postmark from my hometown of Lititz, Pennsylvania, 600 miles away.

More than a year had passed since I had traveled there for my father's funeral. Occasional sympathy cards still appeared from unexpected corners of my childhood. Old neighbors and friends who had offered a kind word after my mother's funeral 23 ago were thoughtful enough to do so again now that Daddy was gone.

With a pensive sigh, I sliced open the envelope in hand. Ah—better than a greeting card: a gentle, rambling letter filled with news from home, seen through the eyes of a woman who had watched 80 springs come and go. She mentioned my father, of course, and offered her condolences.

Near the end she wrote, "While I was cleaning my desk drawers, I found this and thought you might want it. I had no idea she was so young when she died."

She?

A knot of apprehension tightened in my throat as I picked up the discarded envelope. Out fell a small, white card with a gold cross embossed on the front: *In Memoriam.* I opened the card with trembling hands, certain whose name would be printed inside.

Elizabeth. My mother.

Tears came suddenly, painfully, as though squeezed out of my heart by a rough hand. Too overwhelmed to call out my husband's name, I simply bent in two and gave in to the sorrow, smoothing my fingers over the long-lost funeral home program as though it were my dear mother's hand, fragile and pale.

The message inside the card was brief, stark: *Born. Died. Interred.* A lifetime reduced to places and dates.

She had died too soon in so many ways. Too soon for my father. Too soon for her six children. And especially too soon for me—her youngest daughter, her prodigal.

When my mother left this earth, I was deeply immersed in the risky world of alcohol, drugs, and promiscuity. I had traded away a good-girl upbringing for a bad-girl lifestyle. Shaky times and then some.

Four years later, when my life took a dramatic turn for the better, Mom was no longer alive to see that miracle for herself, to see the difference a relationship with Jesus made, even in a heart as hopelessly broken as my own.

Now, two decades later, one question still tugged at my conscience: Did she die thinking she had failed as a mother, that my poor choices were somehow her fault? Oh, Mom.

I knew better. It had been my doing and no one else's. My own rebellious nature, honed by feminism and sharpened by selfishness, was fully to blame. Only God's love could have softened my hard heart. Only His Word, like a double-edged sword, could have cut through my thick skin, penetrated my innermost thoughts, and changed my life completely.

My father had rejoiced in my transformed life and my unshakable faith. But he hadn't understood, not really. "Good for you," he often said.

No, Daddy. Good for Jesus.

Now their graves are side by side in the cemetery behind

the church in Lititz, where every Easter the congregation gathers at dawn to herald the risen Savior, following the example of Mary Magdalene so many centuries ago.

I closed my eyes and pressed my mother's memorial service program against my heart. My mother had not seen the Lord change my life. But He had done so just the same. Her years of steering me through the doors of my hometown church had not been in vain. However far I had wandered, our Savior had wooed me home.

He is risen, Mom. He is risen indeed.

"News from Home" by Liz Curtis Higgs first appeared in the March/April 2002 issue of *Today's Christian Woman*, a publication of CTI, Inc.

LIZ CURTIS HIGGS IS AN INTERNATIONALLY KNOWN SPEAKER AND THE AUTHOR OF 19 BOOKS, INCLUDING MAD MARY: A BAD GIRL FROM MAGDALA, TRANSFORMED AT HIS APPEARING. SHE AND HER HUSBAND, BILL, HAVE TWO CHILDREN AND RESIDE IN LOUISVILLE, KENTUCKY.

JOYCE WILLIAMS
THE END OF MYSELF

I still remember the day we got our first car. I was seven years old. Up to that time our family had been dependent on friends and city buses to get us where we wanted to go. When Daddy drove home that big old 1946 two-toned, green-and-white Nash, my little sister, Jane, and I were so excited we jumped up and down and screamed. Although it resembled a huge beetle rolling down the road, to us it was a luxury limousine. We waved grandly to our neighbors as Daddy turned the car around on our dead-end street and headed out. We had wheels! And it would be a lot easier to get to church.

We grew up dirt poor, and church was our life and entertainment. Everything we did revolved around the church. We didn't get a television set until I was 16—and that was so Daddy could watch baseball games on Saturday afternoons. When nothing was going on at our church, we visited other churches. I loved church. I remember crying at the last service of each revival because I wouldn't get to go the next night. When the speakers and singers left I felt as though I were losing good friends.

I got saved as a young girl. As a matter of fact, I was probably saved a hundred times. The special speakers at my church would never go away saying they had experienced barren altars—because they could count on me! I was usually there—and with good reason.

You see, Jane was one of my biggest problems. We must

have been two of the orneriest kids ever. Together we were a mess. She knew how to push my buttons, and I sure liked to irritate her. Her specialty was pinching and scratching. Mine was biting. One day Mama finally told me that if I bit Jane one more time she would whip me. (Mama didn't spank—she whipped!) So the next time I wanted to bite Jane I warned her (not for her good but for mine), saying, "My teeth are getting mighty bitey!" And she backed off. It was very common for me to lose my religion in the back seat of the car on our way home from church after just getting saved again.

Monday was washday at our house. Mama would roll out the wringer washer and set out the galvanized tubs. She would fill one with hot water for washing, cold water for rinsing, and another one for bleaching. Jane and I loved washdays. Mama was very preoccupied, and we could get away with more mischief. Sometimes we would "run away from home." But we even made that a spiritual journey, because we would go to our church just four blocks away. It was not unusual for Mama to get a call from a neighbor lady who lived next to the church. "Mrs. Bain, do you know where your girls are?" When she found out we were back at the church again, she would come marching down the street with a big switch in her hand to get us. All the way home she would swat our legs, and sometimes she tied us into our little rockers for a while so she could finish the wash.

One of our favorite pastimes was playing church. For whatever reason, I was always the preacher. One Monday afternoon Mama was hanging a load of laundry on the line while Jane and I played church. Our pastor had dedicated a baby the day before, so we decided to reenact that scene. Jane quickly captured our cat while I got ready for "church" by making an aisle between the tubs. When everything was ready the "mother" slowly walked to the "altar" carrying her precious charge. I carefully took him from his beaming care-taker and murmured dedicatory words. Then I proudly held the squirming kitty up for the imaginary congregation to see. Unfortunately, as I turned to make sure everyone could get a glimpse, he leaped out of my grip and fell right into the cold water tub. Thank goodness it wasn't the bleach tub or the hot water tub.

So you can see that I've been a very "religious" person since my earliest years. As I grew up, I became active in all church activities. Youth camp was the highlight of my year. One year I was voted "Miss Virginia" for our all-state teen camp. Several times I was elected leader of our youth group. In high school I was elected president of the Voice of Christian Youth and of the Bible club.

I distinctly remember the day at missionary convention when the Lord called me into full-time Christian service. I was 15 years old, and it was exciting to anticipate what the Lord had in mind for my life.

Upon graduation from high school, my lifelong dream of going to Trevecca Nazarene College in Nashville was fulfilled because of scholarships and the help of friends. Although I did and said the right things, I must confess that my spiritual depth was somewhat shallow.

Sadly, my dear daddy died in the middle of my sophomore year, and I had to leave school. Running ahead of God and the call He had on my life, I married a young man I had met at college. We both became active in my home church in Roanoke, Virginia. Four years later, our first daughter, Tami, was born, and Bethany joined us 18 months later.

From all appearances we were living the American dream. But the truth was that our family was extremely dysfunction-al. I was the ultimate codependent enabler. We had to look good! How could such wonderful pillars of the church ever admit to problems? So I covered up—and we kept running fast and furious—many times ahead of God's plan.

And we did church. That's all we had ever known. Our activities intensified. It was very gratifying to be a member of the church board. I was thrilled to be selected as the pioneering Women's Ministries director for the Virginia District. Later, when I was the first woman in our denomination to be elected to a district advisory board, I felt very fulfilled.

However, all my activities and involvements really hindered my family time and private devotional moments. I found myself so preoccupied with church activities that I confess there were times when I chose those activities over time with my family. When my daughters were in high school, I was offered a management position at work. My schedule intensified. We were living in the fast lane—plus!

Then life as I knew it came to a screeching halt. The facade ruptured, and I could no longer hide the truth. After almost 26 years of marriage, my husband informed me—on the way home from church on a Wednesday night—that he didn't love me and probably never had really loved me. He had found someone else—again—and wanted out of the marriage.

I had heard this story from him 12 years earlier, but reconciliation and restoration had taken place. However, this time there was a note of finality, and I sensed that my greatest fears were becoming reality. I was in the grip of anguish, and a storm had begun to rage in all of its fury, battering and buffeting from all sides.

In a fog of despair I groped my way through the next day, and then the next. I had finally come to the end of myself. Two days later I was driving home on the Blue Ridge Parkway barely able to see the two-lane road through my tears. As I approached a long bridge, to my amazement I began to hear a voice inside me whispering, *You know—there's a way out of this* pain. *Remember that as you begin to cross that bridge there's a little unprotected area with no barrier. You could just turn the wheel, and the car would plunge hundreds of feet into the gorge below. It would all be over.* To my horror I found myself beginning to edge toward the side of the road. Then sanity returned, and I quickly straightened the wheel. Once across the bridge, I stopped the car for a moment and thanked the Lord for guiding me. How dare Satan tempt me with suicide! The anger I felt at his audacity shifted my gloom, and my heart lifted a little as I drove home.

Later that night, as I cried out to the Lord for help, I began to realize for the first time in my life how spiritually malnourished I was. What about my faith? There was no doubt that I was a believer. But now that my life was shaking on all fronts, how strong was my foundation? Although I knew the right things to say and the words to every verse of many hymns, I had to acknowledge that I needed help. I pulled out a simple hardback Bible (not my pristine, going-to-church, leather-bound Bible). It had wide margins, and I began to devour it as I journaled around the scripture passages. In the ebb and flow of a dying marriage and disintegrating family, I found myself enmeshed in the Old Testament as I absorbed the Psalms, Job, and Isaiah. Those books of the Bible had always been familiar acquaintances, but now they became close personal friends.

Over the next few days and weeks as I prayed, read the scriptures, and cried out to God, He began to peel away the layers of my piety. I felt bare and exposed as I honestly faced who I really was—and why I had "done church" so avidly for so many years. I felt that the pain was unbearable. With honest introspection I cried out, *Search me, O Lord.* Sure, I had been a Christian since I was eight years old, had done many good things, and had even led a number of people to the

Lord. But as the Lord's searchlight honed in on my motivation for some of my church involvement, I had to truthfully acknowledge that, although I did many things for God and the Kingdom, there were times when I had been seeking personal fulfillment and praise from those around me. To this day, it's difficult for me to acknowledge this. And I confess that I still have to be on guard and constantly evaluate my motivation.

Day after day, the torturing reflections continued. At times I felt as though nothing would be left of me. I was stripped to bare bones spiritually and emotionally. As I struggled to keep my job going, plan Bethany's wedding, and perpetuate the facade of my marriage—since only a small handful of friends knew about the affair—I teetered on the verge of a breakdown. Some days it looked as though reconciliation would take place, but then he would change his mind. In my agony I cried out to the Lord over and over but found myself still trying to take care of things myself. It was an insane time.

One night I finally fell on my face and cried out to the Lord with David, *"Cleanse me with hyssop, and I will be clean; wash me, and I will be whiter than snow. . . . Create in me a pure heart, O God, and renew a steadfast spirit within me"* (Ps. 51:7, 10). As I prayed, *Father, forgive me for my selfish ambition—re-make me, remold me,* it felt like Mama's washday all over again as He cleansed me. I felt the pruning fork of His grace and the paring knife of His love peel away the last remnants of self-seeking aggrandizement. Years of striving to be perfect, to do it all, to be everything to everyone fell from my shoulders. Purged, cleansed, and renewed, I prayed again with David, *"My soul clings to you; your right hand upholds me"* (Ps. 63:8).

As I knelt there, I was reminded of Mama's switchings. I determined that, by God's grace, I would quit "playing church." Somehow, although I recognized there was still a trail of tears to traverse, I knew that tomorrow's path would be purer. Instead of running away to church as Jane and I had done as children, I determined to be still and wait for His plan.

My shaky faith was replaced with rock-solid confidence. With new assurance I rose to take the next step into the minefield of living with infidelity and the quagmire of a fractured home—upheld by His righteous right hand.

JOYCE WILLIAMS, THE COMPILER OF THESE STORIES OF UNSHAKABLE FAITH, AND HER HUSBAND, GENE, ARE FOUNDING DIRECTORS OF SHEPHERDS' FOLD MINISTRIES, A MINISTRY OF ENCOURAGEMENT FOR PASTORS AND THEIR FAMILIES. THEY WORK FREQUENTLY ON SPECIAL ASSIGNMENTS FOR THE BILLY GRAHAM EVANGELISTIC ASSOCIATION. THEY LIVE IN WICHITA, KANSAS.

FAYE KOKER

I'M ON A JOURNEY

As I stood at the sink washing dishes that February morning in 1975, the shrill doorbell startled me. I quickly dried my hands and hurried to the door. Two men from my husband's plant stood there—with news I could not comprehend. In hushed tones, they told me that there had been an explosion and that Dale, my husband of 28 years, had been killed instantly. The rest of that day is a blur. But late that night when I went to bed, I remember that I cried and tossed and turned, wondering how my four children would survive this loss. Our daughters, Janet and Dalene, were grown, but our boys, Richard and Ron, were just 6 and 14.

Finally, in the stillness of that night, God reminded me of the words He had spoken to me just a few evenings earlier as I was having my devotions. In my heart I had heard His still, small voice gently telling me that I would be going through a time of great sorrow and trouble. But then He had whispered ever so softly that I would not be overwhelmed. He said, *"Never will I leave you; never will I forsake you"* (Heb. 13:5). He told me that I was not to look at this time but to look beyond, for it would be more marvelous, glorious, and wonderful than I could know.

He reminded me that even though Dale was gone, He was still with us and had promised never to forsake us. The Spirit of the Lord took over and comforted my heart. When I finally drifted off to sleep, He gave me a beautiful dream of bright light shining through the clouds. And I saw a fleeting caption reading, "Critical for a moment, then all will be bright." I felt covered with God's peace and was assured that Dale was with Him. My faith soared on eagle's wings.

The funeral was very hard, but God was very close, and He brought me through. Two weeks later, my mother entered the hospital critically ill. Then, one month to the day after Dale died, I was diagnosed with breast cancer. Again, I felt the comfort of God's words: *Don't be overwhelmed—I'll never leave or forsake you.* My faith never wavered.

The doctor told me that I needed a radical mastectomy immediately and would be in the hospital for two weeks. Again, our Heavenly Father took care of my children. As I recovered, He provided everything that we needed and enabled me to raise my sons for His glory. Although there were difficult times, I was never overwhelmed, and our Father was constantly with me.

Eight years after Dale's death, Dalene introduced me to John Koker, who had lost his wife to cancer. After a whirlwind romance, we were married in November 1983. We've had 17 great years together.

In October 2000 I was diagnosed with metastatic pancreatic carcinoma. One of the first things I did was to pull out my notes from years ago when the Lord promised that He would never forsake me. And He never has. He reminded me that I'm on a journey and that He walks beside me every step of the way. My faith is stronger than ever.

The hardest thing I've had to deal with—more difficult than the excruciating pain—is the thought of leaving my loved ones and causing heartache for them. Again, my Father reminded me that we're all on this journey. Some of us just get home sooner than the rest. Then He gave these thoughts to me:

One Generation to Another

Keepsakes and memories of loved ones gone before,
Little things to remind of the past,
Of a love that will always last.
Memories . . . what will be the memories left for us,
Things made and given with love to share
Just so that we would know there was care:
A Bible, a picture, a box, something pretty made,
A smile, a tear, a wink, a hug?
No, Christ's love that came to my heart
Is the greatest gift that I could impart.
The experience of sins forgiven
Jesus has a perfect place for us in heaven.
A wise boy once said, "Don't tell me—show me."
Live your life in what you do
So everyone will know that Jesus touched you.
Let Jesus have first place.
Soon we will see Him face to face.
For the greatest memories of all are forgiveness and love.
(March 24, 2001)

FAYE KOKER WAS A GREAT PRAYER WARRIOR AND A BLESSING TO EVERYONE WHO KNEW HER. SHE COMPLETED HER JOURNEY ON THE NATIONAL DAY OF PRAYER, MAY 3, 2001.

BETH MOORE

BELIEVING GOD

The reason some people find it so difficult to have faith in shaky experiences is because they've never come to truly believe God. Many are afraid not to believe but have not put their total trust in God's Word, His promises, and His power. To acknowledge this is very hard for a "believer." Sometimes we tend to speak in paradoxes as did the father in Mark 9:24 who had a son who was possessed by an evil spirit. When he encountered Jesus, his response to Jesus' promise that "Everything is possible for him who believes" (v. 23) was "I do believe; help me overcome my unbelief!"

I remember when the Lord nailed me on this issue. It happened at a time after I had just entered my fourth decade of life. By that time I had been a Bible teacher, writer, and speaker for a number of years. So how could I possibly admit that although I absolutely believed in God, there were times when I struggled with "believing" God? A genuine journey through honest introspection revealed that I fell into the category of "ye of little faith."

Oh, I prayed—and I studied the Word fervently. But I believed God for way less than He stood willing to do. I found myself praying "safe" prayers—never going far enough out on the limb of faith where the true mettle of God's promises is proven true.

This is especially true in tough times. It's absolutely essential that we establish the validity of our faith during the "trouble-free times" (whenever that might be!). If we do, then when the storms of life sweep over us, we can trust God to keep us from going under. In His time He'll say, "Peace, be still!" as He calms the wind and waves.

You can believe me when I tell you that God wants us to have a faith that will totally set us free to enjoy the life that He's planned for us. He is able to hold us steady, regardless of what's going on around us.

That faith-searching time radically changed my life. Believing God became a lifestyle. You might say, "Well, I guess things were just perfect for you from that moment until now." Not! Some of the best and worst passages in my life have occurred since then. And again, I must confess that we face new challenges to believe God during the changing times of our lives. God specializes in moving us out of our comfort zones. But the reality is that there is never a situation that will come into our lives when God will prove himself to be unworthy of our rock-solid, unmovable faith that He will keep His promises.

Jesus took that boy by the hand and raised him up—delivered and whole! But that's not the only miracle I believe happened that day. I feel confident that this father's faith moved into a different realm, and for the first time in his life, he truly believed!

Don't you know that this father and son never stopped talking about that day? How about the wife/mother? Someday in heaven I want to talk to her to hear the rest of the story!

BETH MOORE IS AN INTERNATIONALLY ACCLAIMED SPEAKER, BIBLE TEACHER, AND PROLIFIC WRITER. HER BEST-SELLING BIBLE STUDIES AND SPEAKING ENGAGEMENTS CARRY HER TO ALL CORNERS OF THE UNITED STATES. SHE AND HER HUSBAND, KEITH, HAVE TWO DAUGHTERS AND RESIDE IN HOUSTON.

JOYCE WILLIAMS
HEAVENLY HUSBAND

I now had no choice but to admit that my home was fractured. Every day brought new grief and fresh pain as my nightmare continued. Some days I saw a glimmer of hope only to plummet to the pits again. Finally, one terrible Saturday he moved out. I could barely see his red pickup truck pull away through my tears.

That evening I cried without restraint. I've always expressed my emotions with tears and could probably qualify for the position of town crier. Even after I went to bed I sobbed into my pillow. Finally, in the early morning hours, I cried out in despair, *Father, this is too hard. Would You please take me to heaven?* And I really meant it. Death would have been so much easier.

Not being the world's most patient person, I gave God about 10 minutes. I remember lying there expecting to see pearly gates and golden streets. When it was obvious that the Father was not going to honor my request, I said, *I can't do this. If I'm to stay and go through this, You're going to have to help me.*

I believe with all my heart that those are some of God's favorite words to hear from us. He had waited almost half a century for my total surrender. For whatever reason, I still recall that it was 3:06 A.M. (I love those digital clocks!) when I turned on the lamp and reached for the Bible by my bed. It fell open to Isa. 54:5-6, and I began to read those precious verses that practically leaped from the page: "Your Maker is your husband—the LORD Almighty is his name—the Holy One of Israel is your Redeemer; he is called the God of all the earth. The Lord will call you back as if you were a wife deserted and distressed in spirit, a wife who married young, only to be rejected."

My tears of anguish turned into swelling joy. My Creator was my Husband! That revelation in the midst of my misery was awesome. From that moment my life was transformed. God revealed himself to me in a way beyond anything I had ever experienced. A divine marriage took place, and He became my Heavenly Husband. I jumped up and began walking through the house communing with the Lord on a whole new level. For hours we talked. I sensed His words of love and comfort. As uncertain as the days ahead appeared to be, there was a calm assurance that my Husband would guide me. As dawn began to break, I knew that His light was shining in my life as never before. My joy knew no bounds, although I was walking in the unknown quagmire of a dying marriage. From those ashes had sprung a heavenly union suffused with hope and illuminated by the light of His love.

My faith increased beyond measure. Although there was "a whole lot of shaking going on" in my life, with my Heavenly Husband holding me steady, I knew I was going to make it.

MILLIE DIENERT
STARTING AGAIN WHEN LIFE STOPS

The doctor's words stunned me. My husband, Fred, had died? *This can't be happening to me,* I thought. *How can I possibly live without Fred?* There seemed to be no way I could face life without my supportive husband, who had stood by me for more than 54 years.

For years as I spoke to various groups, my message was, "When the worst happens to you, when the time comes that you have to endure what you swore you never could, there are always the promises of God. They are safe to trust and the only security you can count on."

I leaned on the Lord and His promises through many family traumas. But Fred had been with me. Now he was gone. It seemed as if my life had ended. Somehow I got through those excruciating days. Soon, however, I found myself leaning increasingly on my only son, Ted. He assured me I could call him at any time, day or night. And I did. I felt blessed of God to have him.

On my birthday four years later I called Ted at his office and heard a tremendous amount of confusion in the background. To my horror, his secretary told me that he had been rushed to the hospital. Frantically, I called the hospital to learn the devastating news that Ted had been pronounced dead upon arrival. Once more, my life stopped.

It wasn't long before I realized that I had been leaning on

the Lord—plus. Plus my husband, my children, my lifestyle, my speaking, my friends. Two huge "plusses" had been snatched from my life.

Although I was hurting deeply, as I began to totally lean on Him, the Holy Spirit's still, small voice spoke to my heart and told me what I needed to hear and learn each day: *God is not dead; He died for you in the person of His Son for your sins, and you have received Him as your Savior. He has become your Redeemer and your Lord. Lean on Him. Learn to lean on Him and Him alone. Never again look for a "plus."*

In the years since those tragic losses, I have leaned on many promises, especially Eph. 3:20—"Now to Him who is able to do exceedingly abundantly above all that we ask or think, according to the power that works in us" (NKJV).

And it started with the next step. I needed security, something to wipe out the continual, rapid pulse and heartbeat that almost brought me to physical collapse. I needed something to hang on to. By God's grace I came to love the word "now"—even the miserable, anguishing, empty "now."

"Him who is able." I certainly wasn't able, so I didn't try to be. In those few words I learned what it really means to lean on Him and His Word.

"To do." Every time I felt inadequate, insufficient, and unable to do anything—even to get out of bed and get dressed, let alone out of the door—I leaned on Him.

"Exceedingly abundantly above all that we ask or think" and the last line says it all: "according to the power that works in us." Jesus' promise is that He is able to transmit to you all the power you need for any demand you have to face today. That's because you have Him in your life. Trust Him!

When I came to learn to truly lean on Jesus as the supplier of all my needs, I learned about the way He supplies. He provides sufficiency, His way. By trusting Him, leaning on Him, my life is filled with a trustworthy presence and source of leaning.

I learned that in leaning I could be filled with the security I needed in the absence of a husband and a son—through His Word. With that comes the knowledge that His Word is the only thing in this world that will never pass away.

As I learned to truly lean on His Word, it became my source of being filled—although not yet to overflowing. That process is a long one. When we believers lean so heavily upon Him that the full-to-overflowing spills onto the lives of others, we have learned what is the epitome of leaning.

My goal is to discipline myself to be dependent upon God's promises as a daily spiritual tranquilizer. Then, although life may try to stop me, I can begin again.

MILLIE DIENERT IS AN INTERNATIONALLY KNOWN SPEAKER, WRITER, AND BIBLE TEACHER. SHE WAS NAMED "1990 AMERICAN CHURCHWOMAN OF THE YEAR" AND HAS COORDINATED PRAYER FOR MORE THAN 1 MILLION PEOPLE IN 106 COUNTRIES. SHE AND HER LATE HUSBAND, FRED, BEGAN WORKING WITH THE BILLY GRAHAM EVANGELISTIC ASSOCIATION MORE THAN 50 YEARS AGO. SHE IS THE MOTHER OF TWO LIVING CHILDREN AND RESIDES IN BLUE BELL, PENNSYLVANIA.

PEGGY BENSON
I FORGOT I HAD IT—
'TILL I NEEDED IT

was married to a great guy for 35 years. Bob was a wonderful husband, father, pastor, publisher, poet, and speaker. It was a great joy to be his girl Friday. The salary was pretty fair, and the benefits were out of sight, as my grandchildren would say. My job was to type the manuscripts and take care of correspondence. I also went with him when he spoke at retreats, conferences, and churches all over the country. It was a fine life.

It's been 15 years since Bob's journey to heaven. To say I still miss him is an understatement. Since his death, however, God has opened many doors for me to speak. Everyone who's acquainted with me knows that I'm a natural-born talker. But there's quite a difference between talking to friends and family and speaking before an audience. I always thought that public speaking should be left to the professional, the educated, the qualified. I remember wondering how God could possibly use me to do His work.

If I've learned anything these past 15 years, it's that God uses His children to tell His story to His children.

It's a privilege to talk about my journey as a Christian. I've come to expect that once I open my heart and begin to share with a group, it frees the listeners to open their hearts and share their experiences as well. I've heard some wonderful testimonies—stories of real heroes and heroines, of courage and faith, of God's grace and power to change lives.

Persons I encounter are finding hope and peace, mercy and grace, comfort and joy for their journeys. I believe that each of us has something in our lives that we really struggle with. It may be a broken heart or spirit, maybe a broken marriage or wayward child, or it could be a failing body or empty pocketbook. Sometimes hopes and dreams are shattered. I also believe that God calls us as the Body of Christ to help "bind the broken."

When Bob died, I was full of questions. He was 56 and I was 52. Three of our children still depended on us. I couldn't understand why this good man who loved God had to die.

But God had a plan. For Bob there was total healing; for me there were new ways to serve, new areas of life to explore, and new goals to strive toward. There came a new awareness of the pain of others and an opportunity to give of myself. God began to use me to reach out to others and to receive the blessings and comfort they offered in return.

Recently I've lived every mother's nightmare. My son Tom died in a fall from a 150-foot bluff. Once again I've drawn strength from God and His children, and once again I draw healing from sharing the brokenness of my life with those who know about brokenness. It's balm to my spirit to hear stories of courage that others share with me. Faith is contagious, and I've seen the face of God in their eyes.

I was a child of the church all of my life. I remember words and phrases I heard our pastor use and the testimonies of the saints, especially on Wednesday nights during prayer service. Words like "hope," "peace," "contentment," "joy," "faith," "comfort," and "grace," which used to be "their" words. But now, through the broken places of life, they're mine too. I've discovered that they're much more than just words—they're words we can live by and die by, that sustain us in the darkness of life. I recall the testimonies of the saints, and I can almost hear them and see their faces as they pop up across the congregation. "God is faithful. In good times and in the bad, in our successes and in our failures, in our pleasures and in our pain, in the darkest nights and the brightest mornings of life —He is faithful!" And everyone said, "Amen!"

Because He has chosen to dwell in us, we're offered the gifts that come with that privilege, and being His trusting children gives us faith to believe that He can take the brokenness we bring to Him and that He'll take it, bless it, and break it and allow us to share it with those who need renewed courage, hope, and faith.

Through all the moments of my life, the brightest of days and the darkest of nights, I've been at home in my Heavenly Father. I know where my hope, my joy, and my comfort come from. My faith has found a resting place. I discovered faith I didn't even know I had until I needed it—and that's all I need to know.

PEGGY BENSON IS A WELL-KNOWN WRITER AND SPEAKER. SHE SPEAKS REGULARLY FOR "FRIENDS CONFERENCES" AND SHARES CANDIDLY FROM HER LIFE EXPERIENCES. SHE HAS FOUR LIVING CHILDREN AND RESIDES IN NASHVILLE.

ROSANE MACHADO
THE MOST BEAUTIFUL
OF JEWELS

It was a sweltering, humid day in the southern part of Brazil. As the wind drifted lazily through the coconut palms, two men riding their horses to the general store for groceries decided to stop for a rest by the bushes in the shade of a grove of trees. As they relaxed they heard a strange mewing noise coming from the field behind the bushes. They thought that a cat must have hidden her kittens there, and, because it was so hot, they decided to rescue them and give them water.

What they discovered, though, was not baby kittens but a newborn baby girl, still attached to the placenta and umbilical cord. Her mother was nowhere in sight.

The men picked up the infant and took her to the general store. A midwife was summoned, and she tied off the cord and bathed the baby. My cousin was in the store and saw the baby and went home to tell his mother what had happened. My aunt called the police and told them that she wanted the baby to give to her sister.

I was that baby, and her sister became my mother.

When I was a little girl I was told this story. Because of the circumstances of my birth, my early years were filled with feelings of rejection and hopelessness. I was told that nobody loved me, and I wanted to die. My life was empty, and I barely existed. One day when I was 14 I went to church and heard about Jesus. That very day I asked Him to come into my life, and for the first time ever I didn't want to die.

I still found myself dealing with rejection, however. When I finished school at the age of 18, the Lord called me to attend the mission school. That was an enormous challenge, because my parents weren't Christians, and they didn't like the idea. But my friends prayed with me, and the Lord changed my parents' hearts. I attended the mission school two years. Then I met a wonderful missionary pastor, and we were married. The Lord blessed us with three wonderful children—first a daughter and then, only ten months later, premature twins. With our growing family and our ministry, life was very full. We were busy all of the time.

Although God had blessed my life in so many wonderful ways, deep down inside I still dealt with the rejection that had followed me from the early days of my life. So even though I knew that God loved me, and I was in charge of women's prayer meetings and traveled with my husband teaching in many places, I still felt empty inside.

After 15 years of ministry, I went to a prayer conference in Rio de Janeiro. During a prayer meeting the leader came to me and said, "I have a scripture for you. I know it's for you, although it doesn't make any sense to me." Then she read Ezek. 16:4-7—

> On the day you were born your cord was not cut, nor were you washed with water to make you clean, nor were you rubbed with salt or wrapped in cloths. . . . you were thrown out into the open field, for on the day you were born you were despised. Then I passed by and saw you kicking about in your blood, and as you lay there in your blood I said to you, "Live!" I made you grow like a plant of the field. You grew up and developed and became the most beautiful of jewels.

I read the scripture. Then I read it again. I cried until there were no more tears. All the feelings of abandonment and rejection left me. I wasn't the despised project of a man or a woman—I was a beloved and beautiful jewel in God's hands!

In October 2000 I was diagnosed with colon cancer. After surgery, while I was still in the hospital, the doctor told me that I needed chemotherapy treatments since the lymph nodes were involved. I felt as if the whole world had once again crashed onto my head. A new death sentence had been assigned to me. At that moment I once again felt alone, abandoned, and rejected. I cried out to the Lord, *Jesus, help me!*

Then the answer came to me through the same scripture I had been given before. I remembered the words "Then I passed by and saw you kicking about in your blood, and as you lay there in your blood I said to you, 'Live!' . . . I gave you my solemn oath and entered into a covenant with you . . . and you became mine" (Ezek. 16:6, 8).

Then and now, the words of God are a healing balm for my soul. And as His precious jewel, I want to shine for Him.

ROSANE MACHADO AND HER HUSBAND, MARCELLO, HAVE SERVED IN MANY ASPECTS OF MINISTRY FOR MORE THAN 30 YEARS. SHE VOLUNTEERS WITH VICTORY IN THE VALLEY, A MINISTRY TO CANCER PATIENTS. THE MACHADOS HAVE THREE CHILDREN AND RESIDE IN SANTA CRUZ DO SUL, BRAZIL.

JOYCE WILLIAMS
ALL FEAR IS GONE

*T*he Lord had touched me and revealed himself to me as my Heavenly Husband. I remember vividly the next time God responded to my need in a miraculous way.

It was a hot July day, and my daughter Tami had recently left on a mission trip to Canada. My other daughter, Bethany, was now married. I had driven to Richmond, Virginia, to attend a district advisory board meeting for my denomination. As I headed home, the sweltering heat seemed to melt the shimmering ribbon of highway stretched out before me. Then it occurred to me—I would be alone in the house that night. My heart began to beat a little faster.

I had been fearful as a child. My daddy was virtually uneducated and, even though I enjoyed the wealth of loving Christian parents, we were barely able to make ends meet. We moved at least once a year, and many of the places we lived were kind of scary. Some nights I would ask Mama to walk through the house to make sure no one was there to "get me."

This fear had permeated my adult years as well. As I drove along the highway that day, thoughts of being alone in that big house overwhelmed me. On the outskirts of Lynchburg, Virginia, I found myself praying that now-familiar prayer, *Father . . . Husband . . . I can't do this. There's no way I can stay by myself tonight. It's too hard.* Then I cried out, *Would You please help me?* On that sweltering July day I believe God smiled as He heard my cry for help.

I was listening to WRVL, the radio voice of Liberty University. The song ended, and I heard announcer Jerry Edwards say, "I have a special scripture today that I believe someone needs to hear." He began to read Job 11:15-29:

"You will lift up your face without shame; you will stand firm and without fear. You will surely forget your trouble, recalling it only as waters gone by. Life will be brighter than noonday, and darkness will become like morning. You will be secure, because there is hope" (vv. 15-18).

Once again, that camp meeting spirit began to swell up within me. Security . . . hope . . . an end to trouble. But there was more. He continued to read.

"You will look about you and take your rest in safety. You will lie down, with no one to make you afraid" (vv. 18-19).

By faith I claimed every word of those promises. My Heavenly Husband had done it again! I felt the fears of a lifetime leave my body, and I could almost picture them floating through the roof of my car. Because of my joyful torrent of tears, I had to pull my cathedral on wheels to the side of the road. For the first time in my life I was truly fearless. It seemed as if a ton of baggage had been lifted from my shoulders. All fear was gone.

Just a few days later I was reading Ps. 34:4 and found a summation of what God had done for me in my car that day: "I sought the LORD, and He answered me. He delivered me from all my fears."

Oh, yes, I had sought Him, and oh, how He had answered! A sweet and wondrous delivery had taken place. By God's grace and enabling power, my faith in God's deliverance was invincible! I knew beyond a shadow of doubt that I would never be paralyzed by fear again.

And my Heavenly Husband had just begun!

COLLETTE McBRATNEY

FACING FEAR

I don't know what scares you, but I'm afraid of heights, the dark, and snakes—just to mention a few. Everyone has fears. And the truth of the matter is that fear can be harmful or helpful depending on our perspective. Sometimes we realize that the best defense against fear is a strong faith.

My mother's death due to a tragic bus accident resulted in overwhelming fear in me. I was afraid of separation and of what tomorrow might bring. She was only 32, and even at 6 years of age I knew that was too young to die.

It's true that none of us knows what any day will bring. My mother's death brought many unwanted changes. The good news is that no matter what we face, God is in control—if we allow Him to be.

Many times God's plans boggle our minds. After Mom's death, we moved to Philadelphia. One day faith came knocking on our door in the form of two women who invited us to attend Sunday School. After their visit, a yellow bus began to pick us up each Sunday morning, and at the age of 9, I invited Jesus to come into my heart and life.

I was delighted when my dad married Marie, one of the ladies who had knocked at our door. I had a great new mom, and life was looking up. Sadly, that marriage ended in divorce after only three years. Divorce is scary, and I felt fear creeping back into my life. Our home seemed empty without Marie.

One afternoon I came home and called out for my brother, Allan. There was no answer—just silence—deathly silence. Fear clutched my heart—and with good reason. I found Allan's lifeless body lying on the wooden floor with a gun lying beside him. Shock and anguish ripped through me. We still don't know if Allan died as the result of an accident or suicide, but my fears began to resurface.

God kindly brought Marie back into my life just when I needed her most. She offered love, structure, and discipline. Marie took me back to church, and faith began to overcome the grip of fear. She loved and guided me as I grew in the Lord. My life stabilized once again, and the solid rock of Christ Jesus became the foundation of faith upon which I ultimately thrived.

My faith in God, the love of a great woman, and the encouragement of my church enabled me to survive the loss of my mother, the divorce of my dad and Marie, and the death of my brother. I clung to Isa. 43:1—"Fear not, for I have redeemed you; I have summoned you by name; you are mine."

I confess that my life today continues to be a journey of faith. Each day brings challenges and potential disaster, but God has been faithful to help me build a business, a marriage, and a ministry. Every time my world gets shaky I hold tight to God's promises, and He keeps me steady.

COLLETTE MCBRATNEY IS A SPEAKER AND COMMUNICATOR AND SERVES AS PRESIDENT OF CCM TRAINING COMPANY, WHICH PROVIDES PERFORMANCE CONSULTING SERVICES TO VARIOUS CORPORATIONS. SHE AND HER HUSBAND, BILLY, RESIDE IN PHILADELPHIA.

MARY WALKER

SHARING MY FAITH
THROUGH CANCER

The birds were singing outside my window, and the sun was shining brilliantly that morning in 1982 when I found the lump in my breast. I was scared. My husband, Skip, had been recently transferred from Detroit to Pittsburgh, and the subsequent months were intensely hectic. I was traveling with Skip as much as possible, working with the builder on the construction on our new home in Pittsburgh, organizing the interior decorating, and coordinating the sale of our place in Michigan. My fingers nervously hovered over the lump that morning as I wondered what to do. I made an appointment with our doctor back in Detroit. Fortunately, my husband had a business meeting there the same day as my appointment.

Skip comforted me as we boarded the company plane for Detroit a few days later. We had flown with the company pilots many times before, and after we greeted them and sat down and buckled ourselves in, Paul, one of the pilots, leaned over the seat and said, "Mrs. Walker, I know you're new in this area [Pittsburgh] and probably don't have a doctor yet. I just wanted to tell you that if you ever need a doctor, both my father and brother are physicians. Don't hesitate to call them if they can help." Then he handed me a piece of paper with their contact information. I was amazed at the timing. We had flown with Paul for years, and I had never known that his father and brother were doctors. Gratefully, I tucked the paper into my purse.

As the engine roared on takeoff, I asked Skip if he had told them I had a doctor's appointment. He answered, "No. They just know I have a business meeting. I haven't told them anything about your appointment." As I settled into my seat, I felt a sense of peace. Although I was facing a shaky situation, I knew that the Lord was already working on the problem.

When we arrived in Detroit for the doctor's appointment, he tried to drain the affected area and then sent me across the street for a mammogram. Since he wasn't pleased with the X ray, he did a biopsy. In the recovery room precious promises from the Bible kept going through my mind: "The LORD, he it is that doth go before thee; he will be with thee, he will not fail thee, neither forsake thee: fear not, neither be dismayed" (Deut. 31:8, KJV). Again, as I lay there, I felt the peace that comes from the assurance that God is in control.

It was obvious when Skip and the doctor came into the room that the news wasn't good: I had breast cancer. Surgery was scheduled for as soon as possible.

As we flew back to Pittsburgh that evening, I said, "Honey, I just can't get over the fact that Paul told us about the doctors in his family when he didn't even know about my problem. Don't you think we should contact them about doing the surgery there?"

Skip replied, "I agree. It's more than a coincidence. I'll call as soon as we get home."

After he explained the situation, he asked Paul's father, "If your wife had breast cancer, what surgeon would you use in Pittsburgh?"

He immediately responded, "Dr. Bernard Fisher. He has the best cancer research program available."

Skip wanted another opinion, so he called the company doctor. He gave us the same answer. We called the doctor back in Detroit, who agreed that Dr. Fisher was one of the best. He was largely responsible for the development of the modified radical mastectomy procedure, which was quite new at that time. So we canceled the surgery in Detroit, and Dr. Fisher accepted me into his program in Pittsburgh. As we were leaving the office, his nurse said, "I heard you mention that you pray. We have discovered that women with faith in God respond much better to this program than those who don't believe."

Skip answered, "Well, there's no doubt—this one here is a believer first-class!" Skip hugged me when we got onto the elevator and said, "We thought we relocated because of my job. The truth is that God moved us here so you would have the best surgeon in the country."

My surgery went well, and the recovery was amazingly smooth. As soon as I was able, I began visiting other patients. When I went into a room where there were no flowers I went back and got a bouquet from the many I had received from friends and family and took them back along with a copy of Four Spiritual Laws in the plastic cardholder. It was a blessing to see the harvest that God gave me right there on that oncology floor! I'm still in touch with some of my fellow patients.

One of my biggest concerns had been that I might have to give up tennis. I was so determined to get back on the court that I played for the first time just one month after surgery, and I actually won a tennis tournament in Phoenix only four months later! I wanted all mastectomy patients to know that life can be good again.

About six months after surgery, Skip and I flew to Norfolk, Virginia, to meet with the reconstructive surgeon. He outlined the procedures, and they sounded good to us. We scheduled surgery. The only catch was that I would have to undergo weekly post-surgical treatments. Skip said, "I don't want her to have that done in Pittsburgh. I'd prefer she be able to recuperate at our condo in Florida."

The doctor thought a moment and then said, "Come to think of it, one of our doctors, Dr. Fishman, has moved to Florida recently and opened a practice there. He's in Clearwater. Where is your condo?" We just looked at each other in amazement. Our condo is just outside of Clearwater in Belleair—right where Dr. Fishman's office is located. God had done it again!

The Lord has used my experience with breast cancer to open many doors for me. I share my experience with cancer patients, with Christian women's groups, and I have an Internet support group. I've enjoyed wonderful opportunities to tell of my faith in Jesus.

Through cancer I've learned to truly trust God in all circumstances. I wouldn't have chosen cancer, but I wouldn't trade the experience for anything else. The Lord has enabled me to share my faith with hundreds and probably thousands of doctors, nurses, patients, and cancer patients' families.

Today, over two decades later, I say, *Thank You, Lord, for orchestrating my life. When my world was shaking, You held me steady. You enabled me to spread my faith to the faithless and offer hope to the hopeless.*

All I can say is *Thank you, Lord, for turning my cancer into a blessing.*

MARY WALKER IS A NOTED AUTHOR AND SPEAKER FOR WOMEN'S CONFERENCES AND RETREATS. HER PASSION IS PERSONAL EVANGELISM. SHE AND HER HUSBAND, SKIP, HAVE THREE CHILDREN AND RESIDE IN CLEARWATER, FLORIDA.

ROSANNE GILMORE

IN HER EYES

This is the story of one little girl
Who never asked to come into this world.
But she was lighthearted and loving and kind.
Her mother said, "A treasure"—one hard to find.
Oh, how she loved all the animals on the farm,
Warm summer days—running to the barn;
Autumn colors and falling leaves,
Brilliant white snow covering the trees.
And don't forget spring flowers growing wild.
Surely, she had to be God's own child.
And I'm certain if you had looked deep inside,
You would have seen the innocence in her eyes.

Then—evil came to that carefree place,
And nothing could have prepared her to face
The malevolent beings that came one night
That destroyed her innocence and put out the light.
The monsters said she could not tell
Or they'd send her mother straight to hell.
So for the next eight years she lived in dread.
Afraid to go to sleep—afraid to go to bed.
She started to give up; nothing really mattered,
Not understanding that her soul had been shattered.
She questioned why she was alive.
You could read those questions in her eyes.

For eight long years she ran and hid.
But sometimes no matter what she did
The evil ones would always find her there.
They'd pull her arms and pull her by her hair,
Kicking and screaming, scratching and biting,
Crying and pleading, dragging and fighting,
A big white pillow to silence her screams,
Take away her breath—destroy her dreams.
Blessed unconsciousness overtook her then.
Her life was not her own to spend.
She wanted to live. She wanted to die.
When she awoke, there was terror in her eyes.

She lived and grew, not as a child should.
Not with kindness or love or anything good.
She grew in spite of the evil things
In spite of the neglect, the beatings, and molestings.
She grew up quickly. She grew up strong.
There didn't appear to be anything wrong.
She grew in the knowledge and ways of this world
And she looked to be normal—an average girl.
But it was all a lie. It was all deceit.
The enemy had come to kill and to cheat.
Because all of her brokenness was on the inside,
Just the few who cared saw the emptiness in her eyes.

Growing up, making all the wrong choices.
Living for today, listening to sinful voices.
Thinking money, parties, fun times, and more
Would bring the happiness she was looking for.
Marrying young was just an escape,
But soon she knew she'd perpetuated the cycle of hate.
Deeply engrossed in her daily life,

Holding at bay the heartache and strife.
Children and home and work took over
Never taking time or getting help to recover.
She could never stop through days filled with sighs.
She had to hide the desperation hidden deep in her eyes.

Her world was dark, her life just a shadow.
It took all of her energy to just not let go.
Terrified of all that he said and all that he did,
Scared of his rage, afraid for her kids.
But she had to keep going! She had to live!
They were so young when she had nothing to give.
The anger, the fear, the hate, and the pain—
That hopeless cycle—there seemed no way to change.
Breathing through one more day, one more night—
Might as well take those pills and give up the fight.
But before she did, she wondered out loud,
What did the Bible say life was all about?
Then she recalled the stories of Jesus the Christ.
And for an instant there was a glimmer of hope in her eyes.

She knelt to pray for the very first time.
Saying, "Jesus, they say that You are divine.
So if You care about someone as wicked as me
You're going to have to prove it, because I can't see
How anything could change my horrible life.
I don't know how to be a good mother or wife.
I only know about the darkness and the dirt.
I only know about pain, about anger and hurt.
Jesus, are You really there?
Show me now—if You truly care."
She bowed her head and started to cry.
With total despair filling her eyes.

A powerful light filled that darkened room
Lifting her from the storms—taking away the gloom.
She looked back and saw all of them there—
Black boiling clouds filling the air.
But she was warm and drawn by the light.
She felt no pain, no fear, and no fright.
Then she saw Someone standing just ahead—
She knew Him! O Lord? Was she alive or dead?
No, no—she hadn't swallowed the pills!
But how could she be here? Oh, it was His will!
He smiled at her and extended His hand.
Shocked by the nail marks, she could hardly stand.
He caught her and said, "I did that for you."
But she cried, "I'm not worth it! How could this be true?"
Savior and saved standing side by side,
Her healing completed when she looked in His eyes.

You see, somewhere outside of time and space
There's a divine appointment, an anointed place
Where Jesus waits for each lost soul
To come to Him and to be made whole.
It's not His wish that any should perish.
He wants all to know they are loved and cherished
By the One from Whom all good things flow.
And now she knows that she knows that she knows
That He is Lord of Lords and King of Kings
Son of God and above all things.
He's the Alpha and Omega and the Morning Star.
Always so close—never too far—
To reach out and wipe away the tears,
To take the hurt, the pain, and the fears,
To make you glad to be alive,
To place His joy, His peace inside.

Look at me if your life is full of sighs,
For I know you'll see His peace in my eyes.

ROSANNE GILMORE IS MANAGING DIRECTOR OF HUMAN RESOURCES FOR THE
BILLY GRAHAM EVANGELISTIC ASSOCIATION. SHE AND HER HUSBAND, DAVID,
ARE PARENTS OF A BLENDED FAMILY OF FOUR CHILDREN. THEY LIVE IN MIN-
NEAPOLIS.

CANDI BROWN
A PERFECT MATCH

And Dr. Cook's daughter has flown halfway around the world to give him a kidney." That's what the television news-caster said that night in March 1995 when I flew in from Papua New Guinea. How crazy is that? We were on television all because of a kidney. But you know, that kidney gave us the opportunity to share our Father's miraculous healing power with many around us and to experience it personally.

In the early 1980s my paternal grandmother was diagnosed with polycystic kidney disease. It hadn't been recognized in its early stages, and it had already begun affecting her other organs, so her doctors prescribed kidney dialysis. Several times a week she was hooked up to a machine that filtered the waste products from her body. Three months later she went to heaven.

Six or seven years later, my dad began experiencing symptoms as well. He was often light-headed and tired easily. I was a college student when he told us he had the same disease that had taken my grandmother's life. Our family cried together. "But," Dad said, "we've found it early enough that someday down the road I'll be a candidate for a kidney transplant."

Just two years later that time came. It was my first year out of college, and I was teaching missionary kids in Papua New Guinea. When I came home at Christmastime, more than 15 members of our extended family met with the transplant team to discuss Dad's impending surgery. Following the meeting, we were all tested to see if one of us could be identified as a possible donor.

I couldn't believe it when the nurse called several days later to tell me that my kidney was a perfect match. I could give him one of my kidneys and save his life! Amazingly, both my brother Chad and my mom, Elaine, were potential donors as well, but mine was the perfect one. With absolutely no hesitation, I said I would do it. We had given Dad and his disease to the Lord years before, and I was just allowing the Lord to use me to carry out His plan. Before I even knew what my role in the procedure would be, the Lord had given me a word from Ps. 27:13-14 that says, "I am still confident of this: I will see the goodness of the LORD in the land of the living! Wait for the LORD; be strong and take heart and wait for the LORD." Through these verses He was telling me that Dad would be OK and that He would give him many more years to be with us.

I know there are friends reading this book right now who have prayed for healing for their loved ones just as fervently as we did, but their prayers weren't answered with physical healing. I'm so sorry. I think about how my family would feel if Dad hadn't been given the chance to receive this transplant and had gone on to be with our Father. I know that even in our grief we would have been grateful for all the wonderful times we had enjoyed with him. But I believe that God is faithful no matter what! Our responsibility is only to trust that He knows what's best for us. For my family, His best was giving my dad more years to live because of his new kidney.

The surgery was pretty rough, but Dad was up and feeling good almost too quickly for my mom! In the years since the transplant, he's had no problems with the new kidney. The Lord's ways are perfect. My dad, who is a physician, has thousands of patients who come through his office each year who have seen how well he feels. One of the local stations carried our story for several weeks, so we had the opportunity to share our faith on television many times.

Now every year on March 27, our family celebrates "Happy Kidney Day," and we recall God's goodness and healing power. These celebrations are never without a few tears, a couple of "remember whens," some laughter, and of course, our prayers of thanksgiving.

Great is Thy faithfulness, O God, my Father . . .

CANDI BROWN IS A GIFTED TEACHER, WRITER, AND COMMUNICATOR WITH A HEART FOR MISSIONS. SHE AND HER HUSBAND, MARK, HAVE ONE SON AND ARE EXPECTING THEIR SECOND CHILD. THEY RESIDE IN OLATHE, KANSAS.

JOYCE WILLIAMS
TEARS IN A BOTTLE

Tears dripped like rain from my eyes
  As trouble's night flooded over me.
My aching soul quivered with fear
  Not a ray of light could I see.

Then God whispered to me softly
  As He drew me close to His side.
He told me with sweet assurance
  "I know each tear that you've cried."

He said, "Child, I really love you.
  Every tear you've shed from your soul
I've collected in My bottle.
  I've caught each drop on My scroll."

"So no tear or sorrow was wasted.
  I've saved all that fell as you wept.
My blood touched each drop in My book.
  And My tears joined yours that I've kept."

Hope returned—sadness turned to gladness
  For I knew my tears weren't alone.
They've been gathered by my Savior
  Kept in a bottle in His heavenly home.

"Put thou my tears into thy bottle; are they not in thy book?" (Ps. 56:8, KJV).

Tradition tells us that when Israelite warriors went off to battle they gave their wives and mothers small vials and instructed them to catch each tear and save it in the bottle. Upon their return they would celebrate the victory and pour out the tears together.

JOYCE WILLIAMS
ROYAL REALTOR

God's amazing deliverance freed me from fear.

You might wonder if I became a paragon of peaceful serenity because of the things God was doing in my life. After all, I had a Heavenly Husband and had become the incredible fearless woman! I wish I could say that I handled every situation exactly the way I should have. But honestly, at times I failed, mishandled situations, and under extreme duress tried to once again take matters into my own hands. During those weeks and months I just about drove my pastor and his wife crazy. They, along with a few close friends, patiently endured my temporary insanities and loved me through them. And my gentle Husband would tenderly chide me as He faithfully continued to rein in my raging type A personality. The absence of fear was a great bonus, but I was still far from perfect.

One of the biggest problems for me was to even allow the D word—divorce—to enter my vocabulary. From my perspective, that had never been an option. Murder, maybe—but divorce? Never! As the death of my marriage loomed inevitably, I was forced to deal with certain cold realities.

There was no way I could continue to live in our house—to pay the mortgage, maintenance, and upkeep on it. The utilities alone were more than I could manage. After several discussions, we decided to list it with a realtor. She told us, "This will be a hard house to sell. It will take a very special buyer to realize its true value."

My home was a charming Williamsburg Cape Cod located in a parklike setting on several acres. As the realtor and I stood in the living room that summer morning, the luster of the hardwood floors shone brilliantly as the sun pierced the pane of the antique front door. We walked through the house, and the realtor said, "I hope you can find somebody who will appreciate the quality of this beautiful house. But it's highly unlikely that you'll find someone who's willing to pay what it's worth." Those could have been very scary words if God hadn't already delivered me from fear.

The very first day after the house appeared in the multiple-listing publication, a realtor called and said he had a client who wanted to see it. I did all of the special things I had been told to do—soft lights, quiet music, cinnamon potpourri simmering on the stove. Then I prayed!

Imagine my amazement when a young dentist and his wife walked in the front door, and she said, "This is my dream house! I've prayed that the Lord would guide us to a house just like this!" The first couple who looked at the house bought it for the full price.

When my realtor brought the contract for my signature, I told her the story of how God had become my Heavenly Husband. She said, "He sure makes a great real estate partner! This one really takes the cake. I never dreamed you'd get full price."

While I stood watching her drive away, it dawned on me that I needed to find a place to live. Where would I go? In a bit of a panic, I called the realtor as soon as she was back in her office. I had a townhouse in mind that would work for me, and I wanted to make an offer on it. But my Heavenly Husband called in my experienced legion of angels from semi-retirement and began to work another miracle.

As soon as I hung up the phone, it rang again. It was the

buyer—the young dentist. He said, "You might think this is a little strange." My heart fluttered a little faster. What was he going to say? Did he want to get out of the contract? Then he continued, "My wife and I have talked it over. We have a home at the lake, and that's where my practice is located. We've decided we'd like to stay there until after the Christmas holidays. Is there any possibility you'd consider living in your house until after the first of the year?"

Excitement welled up within me again. Would I? Live in my own house? But how could I afford it? I then proceeded to tell him the circumstances about the impending divorce. Then he asked, "How much could you afford to pay?" As God would have it, I had just completed my proposed budget and told him the amount I had allocated for rent. He said, "That'll work! You stay right there. We'll take possession after Christmas."

I couldn't believe it! My Husband had already arranged for the sale of the house. Then He made provision for me to stay there. He knew that buying a townhouse would complicate the future He had planned for me.

As a realtor, God treated me royally. Imagine—the King of the universe took time to orchestrate the sale! I'm so glad that I finally learned to listen to that still, small voice.

BRIGITTE GSCHWANDTNER

WHEREVER YOU GO

He wants me to help him on his mission team."

"Does that mean we'll have to move to the States?"

"Yes."

I sat stunned.

It was our 28th wedding anniversary. My husband, Hermann, had just returned from an unexpected two-day trip to New York. I had felt uneasy about this trip from the beginning when his friend had asked to meet him for a reason too important to discuss on the phone. Somehow I couldn't shake off the feeling that our lives were about to be changed in ways that might not prove welcome.

"Nothing's settled yet," Hermann said as he tried to calm me after breaking the news that we might be relocating to the United States. "We need to pray about it and find out what the Lord wants us to do."

I knew he was right. But inwardly I felt numb. I had been born in Germany, raised there, and had lived there for more than five decades. I loved my country, and I especially cherished the area where we lived at the time. My heart was wrapped around the cozy village clustered among the gently rolling hills covered with forests. Every season displayed the trees' gorgeous colors—many different shades of green in spring, and in the fall yellows, oranges, browns, reds, always interspersed with the dark greens of firs and pine trees. I treasured our walks through blooming meadows in spring and early summer. I loved to watch pheasants and hawks and buzzards and many other birds right in front of my window, and I especially enjoyed the view from our living room. Our home was the last one at the edge of the village, halfway up the hill. From our home we overlooked the entire valley—nice, clean homes nestled near a clear, gurgling creek. Behind them the forest climbed up the hill on the other side. In the evenings tall firs stood black against a crimson sky.

For more than 11 years I had called this place home. I felt safe here—and fulfilled. Here I had written most of my novels and enjoyed holding the finished books in my hand. In addition, I was heavily involved in our local church. Suddenly I was to leave all that and move to another continent? At my age?

We discussed the request and prayed, prayed, and discussed. At the time, I had been reading the Book of Joshua in my daily devotions. On the day the decision was finally made, which was to accept the move, chapter 1, verse 9, captured my attention, consoled me, and strengthened me: "I command you—be strong and courageous! Do not be afraid or discouraged. For the LORD your God is with you wherever you go" (NLT). In this time when all that was familiar was being shaken, I was assured that God would give me the faith I needed.

During the following months, while we planned and prepared and tried to get all our papers in order, this promise remained with me and sustained me each time I started to have second thoughts. After all, my husband would have to travel extensively while I would stay alone at home most of the time. Could I endure that in a foreign country? Could I cope with the different language, different mentality, different lifestyle? Could I—rough German that I am—find new friends who would understand my different way of thinking?

Could I find beauty in a big city? Lots of questions danced around in my thoughts. Yet when I concentrated on God's promise, His peace calmed me.

Friends across the States all the way from the Atlantic to the Pacific Oceans wrinkled their noses when they heard where we were going to move. "Kansas? Couldn't you pick a nicer spot? It's so flat!" What a contrast to the beautiful setting in which we had lived so far.

But what a lovely surprise awaited us when we arrived in Olathe, Kansas—our new home was built on top of a hill! It was quite a small hill, I admit, more like a soft-rounded wave on the surface of the earth, but high enough to give us a nice view from the second-floor windows. There's even a creek nearby and a few trees. As a matter of fact, I haven't seen the entirely flat part of Kansas yet.

We couldn't move in right away because the house wasn't ready. Our belongings needed four to six weeks anyway to "swim" across the Atlantic. So we rented a furnished duplex that became available. And the next pleasant surprise awaited us: Our neighbors were friends that we knew from Europe.

We still had many things to adjust to—like using a language for everyday life that I had not grown up with. In Europe we do learn English at school, yes, but we learn British English. So I knew I was in for a good deal of blunders. People still exclaim, "Oh, I love your accent—it's so cute!" Funny—in England they tell me I have an American accent.

But the accent is just a small matter. There are other areas where I'll probably face my limitations. For example, my hair did not stop growing when we left Germany. So I need to go to a—what? Haircutter? Barber? Beauty salon? What's the right expression? And when I sit down in that chair what do I say? What do you call those annoying hairs that keep falling across your eyes and nose and blur your vision? Bangs? OK—I got that. But how do I explain which hairstyle I prefer?

Or worse, if I need a doctor, what am I going to tell him about my problem? My dictionary may be of some assistance. But who wants to see a doctor with a huge book tucked under one arm? The small dictionaries don't offer much medical help. Why did those Babylonians ever have to build that tower and thus confuse the whole world?

A German proverb says, "Never replant an old tree." True, it probably would have been easier to make such an intercontinental move when we were still in our 20s. But is God limited to place or age or language? Never! As with Joshua, He's with me wherever I go!

BRIGITTE GSCHWANDTNER HAS AUTHORED NUMEROUS NOVELS. SHE AND HER HUSBAND, HERMANN, HAVE THREE CHILDREN AND RESIDE IN OLATHE, KANSAS.

NINA GUNTER
TEA-BAGS-IN-HOT-WATER
FAITH

believe that Christians are like tea bags—we're at our best in hot water! There's no way we would ever choose for our faith to be under fire. But when we're in the middle of a trial, we must be willing to suffer wrong rather than to do wrong. I remember so well the day my husband, Moody, and I were seemingly dunked into scalding water.

My position is being abolished? Moody questioned, sitting in stunned silence. *What's going on here? Is this really happening? At this stage in my life? With just a few years left before retirement?* He had just received the unanticipated, startling news in a meeting with other church executives.

It had appeared to us that his service at the denomination corporate level had been effective. As director of the Finance Division, he had implemented workable, practical systems for stewardship promotion and accountability. Grassroots constituents had provided positive feedback about his work. And the 100-plus employees of the department had often affirmed him for his leadership and management style.

That day had started out as a typical one. His schedule included a regular quarterly meeting with other church officers. *This should be brief and routine*, Moody said to himself. *Nothing unusual on the agenda.*

After greetings and sharing usual information, one of the men announced that a restructuring would be effected in two months that would dissolve the Finance Department and eliminate the director's position. Moody was stunned and left the meeting in total shock. There had been no warning before the meeting and no explanation afterward.

That afternoon Moody and I had already been scheduled to close on the sale of our house. Although we had lived there for eight years, we had decided to sell since we traveled extensively. We were downsizing by moving into a townhouse that would suit our lifestyle and accommodate our needs just fine.

As we drove to the lawyer's office for the closing, tears streamed down our faces. Through our anguish we talked about God's faithfulness in leading us to sell our home—even months before the unanticipated job loss.

Church leaders offered Moody another position, but he did not sense it was where God wanted him. Although various opportunities came, nothing seemed to be directed by the Lord. As the long days dragged by, the pain was real and deep, and the waiting was difficult and stressful. Moody was only five years away from retirement with full benefits. Now further ministry, at least for the moment, seemed grim and remote. The basic foundation of our lives was shaken, and our faith was truly under fire. Our tea bags were steeping.

Weeks passed. One day a church official called and offered Moody an assignment as district superintendent. Although this position came with many challenges—unlike those that Moody had faced in a similar position years earlier—God clearly told him that this was a divine appointment. It was God's plan. When I was allowed to remain in my leadership position, the Lord added His loving confirmation.

Incredibly, the next six plus years were some of the most anointed of our ministry. God provided us with amazing opportunities to serve Him. In addition, He miraculously blessed us with our personal investments. When Moody re-tired the district honored him in significant ways.

Most important, many endearing and enduring relation-ships were established with the godly people in our new town. The district grew to unprecedented levels, and the member-ship made noteworthy increases. Goals were exceeded in every area. All budgets were paid in full year after year—a first for that district. One large church avoided total disaster due to Moody's financial expertise and advice along with the cooper-ation and input of a wise pastor and willing congregation.

So in reflecting back on those tough days after the ax fell, I must say that God is good! When our faith is under fire, He says, "Be strong, fear not! Behold, your God . . . will come and save you" (Isa. 35:4, RSV). Moody and I, along with our two sons and their families, continue to serve God faithfully in the church we love. We have learned that when you step out on faith, even when your life starts shaking, you can be sure that God will enable you to land on solid ground.

Like the tea bag in hot water, if we hold onto our faith, we can slowly but surely find God's best for our lives. And He will enable us to flavor the lives of those around us with the pungent aroma of our faith and His love.

NINA GUNTER SERVES AS GENERAL DIRECTOR OF NAZARENE MISSIONS INTER-NATIONAL. SHE AND HER HUSBAND, MOODY, HAVE TWO SONS AND LIVE IN GILBERT, SOUTH CAROLINA.

CYNTHIA SPELL HUMBERT

WEAKNESS IS A GOOD THING

I have struggled with the painful darkness of depression intermittently since childhood. It was not diagnosed or treated until I was in my mid-20s, so I often believed that my painful emotions were related to my poor spiritual performance. I thought that if I just had longer quiet times and prayed more, I could somehow please God enough to overcome my depression. When that didn't happen, I felt angry and distant from God.

Last year I shared my feelings with a friend who had also struggled with depression. God had me ready to hear what she said. "It's not wrong to be weak," she said. "It really is OK! What I've learned recently in the first beatitude is 'Blessed are the poor in spirit, for theirs is the kingdom of heaven.' To be poor in spirit requires knowing that we're desperate for and dependent on the Lord's strength." What a hindrance human strength and self-sufficiency can be! How easily it makes us forget that whether we feel capable or not, we're still needy people. So if you're suffering in human weakness from a God-given tendency, shout, "Hallelujah!"

A large part of "poorness of spirit" is humility. I had thought that my depression had somehow caught God off guard and surprised Him. It was humbling to realize that He

had formed me perfectly for His purpose and that He makes
no mistakes.

That truth finally broke through to my heart and my head
at the same time! In the past, I had been able to acknowledge
that God had used my depression since childhood to teach
me many things. I could apply Rom. 8:28 to the depression. I
knew it had helped me develop a more compassionate heart
as a counselor and that it helped me connect with the pain of
others through my writing and speaking.

But I couldn't see that my continued struggle with depression could have a positive result. It hindered me from being
an energetic wife and mother, and it kept me from having the
drive to write more and invest in meaningful friendships. The
truth is, though, that no matter what my circumstances and
whether or not I understand them, God's love for me is still
faithful, abundant, and constant.

For the first time in my life, I told God, *Thank You for
making me just as I am. . . . I will have faith that You'll teach me
whatever you desire. Even if You never heal me, I'll trust You.*

Those were the most difficult words I ever uttered. But at
last peace came into my heart. It's a comfort to freely pray
and have fellowship with God again. I had allowed my anger
to build a barrier between us and had bought into the lie that
if God loved me enough, He would heal me.

If you've believed that lie because of what you've done in
the past or because of a current spiritual struggle, find hope
and comfort in Heb. 13:5-6—"He has said, 'I will never leave
you or forsake you.' So we can say with confidence, 'The Lord
is my helper; I will not be afraid'" (NRSV). We can have faith
that God will never leave us and that His love for us will never change.

The world tells us that we must be strong to succeed. But
God tells us we're in the right place when we're needy and

weak, because then we stop depending on ourselves and others and turn in faith to Him to provide our strength. So I repeat my friend's counsel to others who struggle: if you're weak, that's great! You're now in a place to faithfully plunge into the unending grace and strength of God. You're right where God wants you to be. Stop fighting it, and rest in His love for you. He desires to be the One who faithfully meets all your needs.

Adapted from Cynthia Spell Humbert, *Deceived by Shame, Desired by God* (Colorado Springs: Navpress, 2001), 168, 183-84.

CYNTHIA SPELL HUMBERT IS A GIFTED SPEAKER, WRITER, AND CHRISTIAN THERAPIST PREVIOUSLY ASSOCIATED WITH MINIRTH-MAIER CLINIC AND WAS A SPEAKER FOR THEIR NATIONAL RADIO PROGRAM FOR SEVEN YEARS. SHE WORKS PRIMARILY WITH WOMEN WHO STRUGGLE WITH ISSUES ROOTED IN SHAME. SHE AND HER HUSBAND, DAVID, ARE THE PARENTS OF THREE CHILDREN AND RESIDE IN AUSTIN, TEXAS.

JOYCE WILLIAMS
A DOOR OF HOPE

*G*od had been faithful to provide just the right buyer for my house. Now what?

Throughout those frantic months I continued to work, although our company was struggling financially. As a midmanagement supervisor, I made two visits to the Pentagon to inform the government about programs we offered. As a matter of fact, I was sitting in a general's office the afternoon before the ground war started during the Desert Storm operation. Another general came to the door and called out into the hall the one with whom I was talking. I could clearly hear them discussing the imminent escalation of the war. I could hardly believe where I was and what I was hearing.

But Desert Storm wasn't the only war that had my attention. My personal war continued to rage as well. Every day I was learning more and more about complete reliance on the Lord. He gave me 2 Chron. 20:15—"The battle is not yours, but God's." I clung to that promise and many others. As a matter of fact, for the first time in my life I truly wore out a Bible—the front and back covers fell off. God's Word was my source of strength and encouragement as never before. I have kept that Bible as a reminder of His faithfulness.

My Heavenly Husband was always faithful to provide just what I needed. I remember buying a new book that came out that year, written by one of my favorite authors, Barbara Johnson, that strengthened my faith enormously: *Stick a Geranium in Your Hat and Be Happy!* I devoured it like a starving beggar and found incredible nuggets. One passage in particular jumped off the pages and into my bleeding heart. The title was typically hilarious: "I Feel So Much Better Now That I've Given Up Hope." When I got to the portion titled "God Uses Trouble to Sweeten Us," I was absolutely amazed at the parallels to my own life: "Life is never perfect [that's for sure!], but Jesus is. And He takes the imperfections—the broken pieces and the messes—and turns them into hope. Remember, no matter what you're going through, it didn't come to stay, it came to pass. You may be living in a parenthesis, but whatever you're going through, it won't last forever."

That was so perfect for me that I just about dropped the book! Then I read on as Barbara listed five steps that all of us take when we totally surrender our circumstances to the Lord.

"CHURN. You feel as though your insides are full of knives chopping you in a grinder."

I cried, *I've been there, Lord!*

"BURN. You literally feel as though you are burning inside."

I've been chewing antacids like candy!

"YEARN. You just ache inside for things to be as they were before you knew about this."

Yes, Lord. Oh, how I yearn for everything to go back to normal—whatever that is!

"LEARN. You talk to others."

Lord, I know I talk way too much—to too many people.

"You learn you're in a long growth process. Spiritual values you learned in the past will suddenly become real to you."

Dear Lord, thank You for my godly heritage.

Then Barbara presented the last stage:

"TURN. You learn to turn the problem over to the Lord completely by saying, 'Whatever, Lord!'"

OK, Barbara—I've done all of these. Then some days I go back and start all over. What's wrong with me? I kept reading:

"Just because you've come through all those steps does not mean that you will not go back to churning, burning and yearning on certain days. . . . CHURN awhile. . . . BURN for a time. . . . YEARN for as long as it takes to move on. . . . LEARN as much as you can. . . . and then TURN it all over to the One who cares for you.

"Right now you have a broken dream. . . . But believe me . . . healing does come."

Thank You, Jesus!—just what I needed to hear today!

"You are making a long journey to becoming whole again, and you have a door of hope ahead! . . . We know our future —and our hope—is in Him!" (Barbara Johnson, *Stick a Geranium in Your Hat and Be Happy!* [Dallas: Word Publishing, 1990], 66-68.).

And I shouted out loud—"I can do this! It's OK if I falter some along the way. I'm going to make it. This mess didn't come to stay—it came to pass! Someday God is going to poke a hole in this paralyzing parenthesis. Although many days it seems as if I'm barely able to peek through the keyhole, I know there's a door of hope ahead!"

MARIETTA COLEMAN
RAISING MY EBENEZER

inally our little girls were tucked snugly into their beds. Prayers were over. We had thanked God for His Son, Jesus; for each other; and for Daddy, who was away from us telling others about Jesus. We had asked for His protection over all of us. After we shared kisses and the lights were turned out, I was finally free to process my thoughts of the day.

On our wedding day life seemed so perfect. I wanted to serve the Lord "full time." Was there any better way to do that than to work alongside this wonderful man God had given to me? I was so excited.

The years of combining school and ministry sped by, and I found many ways to work with my godly husband. Finally, degrees in hand, we could be full-time pastors. There was more than enough to keep us busy, and it seemed obvious that God was blessing our ministry.

Then it happened! My husband was invited to begin a Department of Evangelism at Asbury Theological Seminary in Wilmore, Kentucky. It was very clear at that point why God had led him to complete his Ph.D. He saw this as an enlarged ministry where he could help other young ministers prepare and fill their hearts and minds with the same passion for the ministry that burned within him.

So there we were. He was happily arranging his new office, preparing lectures, and I was—well, I was grumbling. I seemed to have traded a fulfilled life of shared ministry for days filled with bugs, babies, and dirt. More and more invitations came for my husband to go out to various churches for weekend meetings and other events. Right about that time two of our evangelist friends died in plane crashes. So I added *fear* to my list of miseries. Would my husband be next? We were all healthy, but I began to worry about what would happen if the children or I would get sick or hurt while he was away. Many times he took our only car, so how would I get to the doctor's office? Or what if someone broke into our house and stole something or injured us?

The list of fears and "what ifs" sizzled in my mind like bacon frying in a hot pan. So every evening at bedtime I gathered my nightly weapons for defense (telephone, flashlight, hammer, screwdriver, and ball bat). I laid them out carefully and conveniently just in case I needed them. Then I nervously closed my eyes and prayed for sleep.

Finally, one night I cried out to God, *Help me!* It was a simple but earnest prayer. At last I was able to "forgive" God for jerking me out of my happy place of ministry after I had assumed that since He had called my husband to Asbury, He would also open a place for ministry for me as well. God could tell that I was ready to replace fear with faith. And I was ready to acknowledge that His plan might be better than mine.

He answered my prayer. That was the last night I needed to take my arsenal to bed with me. He truly took away my fears and replaced that void with faith. Then He gave me 1 Sam. 7:7-12, which describes a big battle between the Israelites and the Philistines. The Israelites went to Samuel and begged, "Do not stop crying out to the LORD our God for us, that he may rescue us from the hand of the Philistines" (v. 8). Samuel took a lamb and offered it up as a burnt offering. "He cried out to the LORD on Israel's behalf, and the LORD answered him" (v. 9). They won the battle! Then Samuel took a

stone and set it up as a reminder. "He named it Ebenezer, saying, 'Thus far has the LORD helped us'" (v. 12).

That night when God replaced my fear with faith, I knew
that I had won a great battle. I had set up a solid rock of faith
and named it Ebenezer. And I kept saying, "Thus far has the
LORD helped us."

Over and over in the years since that night I've had occasions to return to my Ebenezer to give praise to the Lord for
His help in winning the battle. Some battles were small but
still beyond my ability to fight. Some battles were long, painful, and totally out of my control. But when they were finally
over, I could return to my Ebenezer and say again, "Thus far
has the LORD helped us."

A few months ago my husband, who was long past retirement age, felt led to resign both of his jobs. It seemed to be
the right thing to do. But almost before the retirement parties
were over, he was hired for a new job. This meant a reloca-
tion and many other changes.

Then another horrifying surprise entered the picture for
me: cancer. Impossible! I'm a healthy woman. How could we
bid good-bye to long-time friends, move, change insurance
companies, and fight cancer all at the same time? Fear threatened to overwhelm me again.

But I've come a long way in the past 40 years since I first
set up my Ebenezer. We, along with a host of friends, began to
cry out to the Lord on my behalf, and the Lord answered us.
For the first time in my life I had more than a head knowledge of the phrase "peace that passes understanding." And
that peace stayed with me through the entire experience.
Then I returned to my Ebenezer to say, "Hitherto hath the
LORD helped us" (1 Sam. 7:12, KJV). I'm reminded of the
words of an old hymn that express my thanksgiving better
than I can:

Here I raise my Ebenezer;
> *Hither by Thy help I'm come.*
And I hope, by Thy good pleasure,
> *Safely to arrive at home.*
Jesus sought me when a stranger,
> *Wand'ring from the fold of God.*
He, to rescue me from danger,
> *Interposed His precious blood.*
—Robert Robinson

And, you know, one of the greatest joys I've discovered is that my Ebenezer is raised wherever I might go and regardless of what might happen in our lives. So like Samuel of old, I'm going to refuse to take up my old arsenal of weapons and instead lift up the rock of my Ebenezer—faith in the Chief Cornerstone! He's the foundation that's sure and steady—proven to be totally unshakable in the storms of life.

MARIETTA COLEMAN'S HUSBAND, ROBERT, IS DIRECTOR OF THE SCHOOL OF EVANGELISM FOR THE BILLY GRAHAM EVANGELISTIC ASSOCIATION, GIVING HER THE OPPORTUNITY TO MENTOR MANY STUDENT PASTORS' WIVES. MARIETTA AND ROBERT HAVE THREE CHILDREN AND RESIDE IN SOUTH HAMILTON, MASSACHUSETTS.

LAUREL DAVIDSON

THE MIRACLE OF CHANCE

ord, what are you thinking? Cameron is 19. Christy is 17. Finally, Randy and I are able to see the proverbial light at the end of the tunnel—the empty nest. And frankly, Lord, we're looking forward to it. It's not that we don't love our kids, but we have plans: traveling, quiet dinners, romantic weekends for two. This is a beautiful baby, Lord—all that dark hair and green eyes. He's so tiny. But surely You don't expect us to start over.

Well . . . all right, Lord—but just for a while. Remember: Randy and I have plans.

I had known Chance's mother for years. She was 26 when he was born, and she already had three other children. Tragically, she then made the decision that men and drugs were more important to her than her kids. When she left, care of the three older children was split between the grandparents and an aunt. Chance came to live with us. Thinking this was a temporary situation, we didn't worry about the legalities of it all. We just took one day at a time. It was easy to love the wonderful little baby that God had dropped into our lives. I was naive to think that I could rock him, sing to him, love him, and then give him back when and if the time came.

It wasn't long before I realized that this little bundle had stolen my heart. He was so innocent and precious. How could anyone see him as a burden? We spent the first two years of his life raising him as our own. But because we did not have custody or guardianship, we were forced to hand him over to his father frequently.

After two years of living on shaky ground, we decided it was time to work on establishing legal rights. We went to three different lawyers. All of them said the same thing: without the voluntary consent of the parents, we "didn't have a prayer"—funny choice of words. Evidently they were not aware of the power of prayer.

I've been blessed with a wonderful stepmom, Joyce, who's a true prayer warrior. One evening before our first court appearance, she called to see how I was doing. Through my tears I said, "I need a miracle. We really need to at least get guardianship."

She said, "Well, that sounds good, but I'm praying for adoption."

I laughed, thinking, *She just doesn't have a clue about how the legal system works. Doesn't she understand that the experts have told us that there's just no way?* Obviously I, too, was unaware of the power of prayer.

On the day of our custody hearing, our lawyer walked into the courtroom and asked us to step into the hallway. Chance's mother had failed to make an appearance. However, the father had, and he had presented our lawyer with papers surrendering custody of Chance to Randy and me. Naturally, we were elated. Our lawyer reminded us that adoption was still not a possibility without the parental rights being terminated. We didn't care at that time, though. We were just thrilled to have custody. But God was not finished yet.

Remember my praying stepmom? She just kept praying. And sure enough, one year later, on May 31, 2001, my dad and Joyce joined us at the courthouse as the judge signed the final papers. God had come through—the adoption was final. Chance was ours!

As I look back on those first three years, it's easy to see that the miracle was not just the adoption but also the day-to-day grace God gave us, the wonderful way He carried us, and the people He put into our lives to support us.

Just as I finished writing this, I looked up to see that dark-haired, green-eyed, 4½-year-old boy standing in front of me holding a bouquet of dandelions and saying, "Mommy, I love you."

I'm so glad that God didn't stick to our plan.

LAUREL DAVIDSON IS A GIFTED TEACHER AND WRITER. SHE AND HER HUSBAND, RANDY, HAVE THREE CHILDREN AND RESIDE IN WICHITA, KANSAS.

KAREN ANDERSON

NEIGHBORHOOD BIBLE CLUBS

Ministry to kids? That was about the last thing I wanted to think about. As a home-schooling mother of six, I needed a break from kids—not more time with kids! Yet I just couldn't shake the Lord's prompting that hot Missouri morning.

It was a long summer. The doorbell rang incessantly, and our home seemed to be the hub of activity for the entire neighborhood. To my dismay, I found myself beginning to resent those little faces constantly parading to our doorstep.

Remember, Lord, I told Him, *I need a break from kids.* My husband travels around the world spreading the gospel, and my job of working beside him and raising these kids is a demanding one. Since I home school, I don't have an empty spot in my heart just waiting to be filled by more kids. I never felt called to children's ministry.

It took a whole year for the Lord to soften my heart, and even now I'm not sure exactly what broke me first. It might have been little kids just outside our window using vulgar language. Or it may have been several intense fistfights in our backyard. It began to dawn on me that some of those children did not have the advantage of going to church or Sunday School. Many of them come home from school and watch Jerry Springer. There needed to be some positive alternatives for these kids who seemed to have so much time on their hands. But where could I find the time and energy? Could God really enable me to carry this new load?

One afternoon our 9-year-old daughter, Kirsten, burst into the back door sobbing. As she collapsed into my arms, I asked her, "What's wrong? Are you hurt? Did somebody do something to you?"

Between sobs she said, "I've been thinking about people who don't know Jesus, the poor, and those who don't have homes. Who's going to help them?" I realized that God was talking to my children as well as to me. He was calling, and I knew that He stood ready to enable me to accomplish His plans.

A few days later I was watching through the front window while Kirsten was talking to two of the toughest kids in the neighborhood. After a few minutes both walked away, each with a dollar bill in his hand. When Kirsten came inside I asked her why she had given them each a dollar of her own money. Then she told me that the only way they would agree to listen to her talk about Jesus was if she would pay them. I guess that's one way to evangelize!

That was all the confirmation I needed that God really wanted me to do something. The ideas started to flow. Summer backyard Bible club—a place for kids to come to be introduced to Jesus—videos, Bible lessons, snacks, games, and outdoor sports. I began to get excited about the possibilities, and that made me realize that this was a God thing. I shared my vision with my neighbor Cindy Hill, and we prayed about the idea. It wasn't long before she came to share my enthusiasm, and we decided to start a "Neighborhood Bible Club." We fully believed that God would help us do it.

That first Wednesday afternoon was a little wild, but excitement continued to grow. We found more helpers. Cindy's 16-year-old son, Ryan, became our sports director. Wednesdays in our neighborhood have become special times for the kids. We've shown them a wide variety of Bible and other videos. They love acting out Bible stories and role-playing as we teach biblical truths and principles. It's great fun to see them participating in Bible quiz competitions.

Cindy and I have to admit that hosting a Neighborhood Bible Club can be challenging, but it's tremendously rewarding to see kids receive the love of Christ and develop healthy relationships. We're able to encourage positive character growth and respect for others—including their parents.

Recent statistics from World Vision tell us that we must reach children at younger ages than before. Statistics from many sources confirm that the vast majority of persons who receive Christ do so before the age of 15. The Lord is clarifying a vision of Neighborhood Bible Clubs in our country and around the world. Through them, Christian families could begin to view their own backyards as mission fields to reach out to millions of kids who are lost and dying without Jesus. Cindy and I knew that God could provide all the resources for faithful families who would respond to this challenge. Just look at what He's doing for us!

Cindy and I have noticed that the atmosphere around us is changing. Oh, no—it's not perfect. But we hear profanity a lot less among our neighborhood children, and the number of fights has dropped considerably. The love of God and the truth of His Word are beginning to permeate our neighborhood.

Now when we ask ourselves if it's worth 90 minutes each week and a plate of chocolate chip cookies to reach these kids for Jesus, the answer is a resounding yes! *And next time, Lord, I promise to listen better—and to respond more quickly.*

My faith roots are deeper than ever.

KAREN ANDERSON WORKS WITH HER HUSBAND, MARK, WHO IS THE INTERNATIONAL DIRECTOR OF THE IMPACT WORLD TOUR OF YOUTH WITH A MISSION. THEY HAVE SIX CHILDREN AND RESIDE IN LEE'S SUMMIT, MISSOURI.

JOYCE WILLIAMS

NO LESS THAN ME

God had been so faithful to me, and I was learning to rely completely on him.

Incredibly, I began to feel God's tug on my heart to be in full-time Christian service. He had called me years ago, but I had missed His plan for me. On a special Sunday evening the music group Spiritbound came to my home church in Roanoke, Virginia, for a concert. I don't remember everything they sang that night, but when they began to sing "No Less than Me," I distinctly felt the reinstatement of God's call on my life. In the midst of man's ultimate rejection, God wanted me! I could hardly believe it.

Overcome, I slipped down the back stairs of our church and found a room where I would be alone. In that precious time, I promised the Lord that I would go anywhere, do anything, be whatever He wanted me to be. I would knock on any door that seemed to be swinging open. All I asked was that He would close all the wrong doors and open the right one. I was learning so much about absolute obedience and commitment, and my faith grew stronger every day.

A couple of weeks later, Moody and Nina Gunter came to Roanoke to speak for missions conventions. In keeping with God's plan, they stayed with Nina's niece, Diane, who lived on our small cul-de-sac. Diane and I walked several days a week, and I told her about God's call on my life. She phoned the very next Saturday afternoon to tell me that Moody and Nina wanted to meet with me.

After the Saturday evening banquet, I took my résumé and walked up the road to Diane's. As we sat in her living room, the Gunters told me about several opportunities. One was an administrative position, and the other was in missions. Then, as an afterthought, Nina said, "I have a young pastor friend in Clearwater, Florida, who's looking for a staff person. He needs someone to serve in the area of Christian education and outreach."

I quickly responded, "I could really be interested in the missions job. But I'm sure God would never ask me to be a full-time church staff person. I don't have that kind of experience or training." There I was again—regressing—trying to tell God what I should do. I still had a lot to learn!

On Monday I made calls regarding the possibilities. Then I called Pastor Mark Lancaster in Clearwater. Somewhat hesitantly I told him who I was. It was obvious that he wasn't too interested in this middle-aged, divorcing woman with no staff experience. Then I actually sat back and let the Holy Spirit do the follow-up.

That week Pastor Mark and his wife, Vanessa, participated in their annual pastors and spouses' retreat. My longtime friend Gene Fuller charged the pastors to put a freeze on hiring staff until all budgets were paid in full. After that session, Mark went to him and said, "I heard what you told us today. But I got a call from a lady in Virginia who says she knows you and Evelyn. She called about a possible staff position at our church in Clearwater. What do you think?"

Dr. Fuller replied immediately, "Forget what I said. If you can work it out, have Joyce come down for an interview."

The next morning my phone rang just as I was leaving for the office. It was Pastor Mark. He told me of his conversation with Dr. Fuller. Then he said, "I've talked with several board members, and we would like for you to come down for an interview."

I was still a slow learner at that point, and I somewhat ar-
rogantly replied, "I'm really honored. But you know I don't
have any real experience as a staff person. I've done those
things as a lay leader. Besides, I think I may be working soon
in missions." Oh, I of little faith! God must have been shaking His head.

Thank God—Pastor Mark was persistent. He called again
and asked me to fly down for a weekend. Finally, I realized
that this was an open door. I had promised to step through
any open door with the request that God close all the wrong
ones. So I agreed to go.

I remember my feeling as the plane circled Tampa International Airport. Looking out of the window at the palm trees
and azure blue water of the bay, I thought, *What am I doing
here?* I felt guilty thinking that I was probably wasting the
church's time and money.

Pastor Mark and Vanessa were delightful, and I fell in love
with their daughter, Vicki. The next morning I taught an
adult Sunday School class. Then Mark told me he wanted me
to sit on the platform. Sit on the platform? In front of more
than 300 people? As I sat there on that short pew looking out
at all the people who were looking back at me, I again
thought, *Why am I here?*

During family prayer time I saw a young teenage girl step
forward and kneel at the altar. Without thinking, I slipped
down the steps, knelt, and prayed with her. After the prayer
time ended, I returned to the platform. But something was
very different! Suddenly it seemed that everything had
changed. There appeared to be a radiant glow over the people,
and I felt in my heart, *These are my people*. No one had told
me that might happen. I whispered, *Father, I don't know what
You're doing, but I believe You might really want me to come here!*

Then I remembered—the vote. Pastor Mark had scheduled a board meeting so they could talk with me that eve-

ning. So I prayed, *If the meeting and vote results are favorable, I believe this is where You would like for me to be.*

The afternoon dragged by. We drove around a little. Mark and Vanessa pointed out some potential places where I could possibly live if I moved there. I had very little cash for a down payment, so we drove by mobile home parks.

Finally it was 4:30. The boardroom was crowded with people—20 men and 3 women. The 23 seemed more like 230. They were very kind and gracious to me, although the interview process seemed to last for hours. I have no idea what I said to them or they to me. I do know that I prayed—hard! Then I left the room so they could vote. All of this seemed so unlikely. How could they seriously consider a middle-aged divorcing woman who had never been on a church staff? My heart raced as I waited in the pastor's study. Imagine my amazement when Pastor Mark slipped out to tell me that they had extended a call to me—and their vote was unanimous. That was an absolute miracle!

As I flew back to Roanoke that night, I prayed all the way. *Father, please make it very clear. I don't want to make a mistake.* The next evening I took my home church pastor and wife to dinner to discuss Clearwater. After we talked, they strongly discouraged me. They said, "Joyce, you don't know what a big job that is. And you're in the middle of an incredible transition in your life. It would be better if you waited a year or two before you do anything so radical. You need time to heal." I knew that from every practical standpoint they were right. But there was this divine tug on my heart that I couldn't explain.

Later that night it was down to just God and me. I prayed, *Lord, You know that I want only Your will. Please make it very clear to me. I don't want to run ahead of You or to lag behind.* In that very moment, in the same room where only a few months earlier God had told me that He was my Husband,

He once again gave me a deep peace. All but audibly I could hear His voice saying, *This is My plan for you. Trust Me. Walk through this door.* With my newly awakened solid-rock faith, I knew I had my answer. With trembling hands and tears streaming down my face, I called Pastor Mark and told him I would come. Waves of joy flooded my soul.

The following weekend I took my mother to the cabin that we had tried to sell for several years. It had become mine as a result of the property settlement. I told the caretaker that I was moving to Florida and didn't know when I would be back. He asked, "Are you interested in selling?" I assured him that I was. Then he told me about a couple who had driven through the grounds earlier that week and were considering purchasing a cabin.

When Mama and I got home, I called the couple, and they said they were very interested. On Monday they drove several hours each way to look at the cabin. Then they called that evening to tell me they wanted to buy it! When the wonderful people of Clearwater flew me back down to find a place to live a couple of weeks later, I had a nice down payment. The Lord opened the doors for me to buy a lovely three-bedroom condominium for thousands less than the appraised value. And it was just five minutes from the church! My Royal Realtor was at work again—selling a cabin and locating my condominium. I hardly needed to board the plane to fly home. My heart was soaring!

Giving myself completely to God seemed so little for all that He was doing in return. How wonderful to know that my puny offering of myself—a nobody—was being returned immeasurably more than I would have dreamed. Then He whispered softly to my heart, *Trust Me. I've only just begun!*

I could almost hear the words of that song, "No Less than Me," as they played over and over in my thoughts. And I was so glad I was obedient.

Of all the gifts that I could bring
To gain acceptance by the King,
There's no treasure great enough
To make we worthy of His love.

But when I look around I see
It's not these things He asks of me.
He wants my very heart and soul—
Then my offering will be whole. . . .

It's when I give to Him my all
And I am yielded to His call
It's then my heart begins to see
My Savior wants no less than me.

No less than me I bring to Him
No less than me my offering.
Nothing else that I could bring
As a servant to the King.
All I am is under His control.
His child I know I'll always be
That's why I bring no less than me. *

                —Dale Kropf

PENNI ARNER

WANTED: A WOMAN OF FAITH

*I*f I had seen the job description in the classifieds, I wouldn't have circled it. There's no way I would have considered calling for an interview on that kind of job.

WANTED

Wife and mother. No experience necessary. On the job (and road) faith training. Trust God on a daily basis for every need without the security of home. Travel thousands of miles a year in an RV. Toilet train two boys while going 70 mph on curvy mountain roads. Maintain an orderly, calm, and peaceful "household" while moving from town to town each week. Keep two active boys and singer/husband's laundry fresh. Set up and tear down in RV park after RV park, motel to motel.

Related Responsibilities: When you arrive at your destination, ask the pastor if any couples in the church need counseling. Make it through numerous visits in the homes of pastors and laypersons with minimal damage and breakage by two inquisitive little boys. Carry on intelligent and spiritual conversations with the district superintendent's wife after hearing your four-year-old tell her little girl she's kind of fat. Resist any temptation to crawl under the table when your toddler throws a piece of bread into the hostess's drinking water and yells, "Two points!" Read James Dobson's *Dare to Discipline* in your spare time and respond appropriately. Resist any temptation to hand your host pastor a list when he asks, "Do you need anything?" Note: All who are interested call on God and apply within.

Who would apply for a job like that? But after 14 years in music evangelism, I can honestly say I wouldn't have missed a minute of what God has allowed us to experience. Living a life of faith in the center of God's will is much more fulfilling than I ever dreamed.

Unlike an earthly job, my employment actually lies in heavenly realms. I'm evaluated not by my on-the-job performance but on my relationship with my Employer—Jesus Christ. And that enables me to live what I believe—"My God will supply all your needs according to His glorious riches in Christ Jesus" (Phil. 4:19).

That's how I'm able to begin each road trip with great confidence. I remember one of our earlier jaunts when we set out for the jungles of Mississippi with the RV packed to the hilt and a seven-week-old baby in tow. OK, maybe it wasn't the jungle, but it was certainly heavily wooded and remote. It was a long drive over steaming roads. Chauncey wasn't eating and was obviously having acute intestinal distress. When Brian pulled into a parking area so he could call to find the nearest hospital, I admit that my faith was a little shaken. He returned within a few minutes with a lady whose RV was parked next to ours. Her first words when she walked into our home on wheels were "OK. I'm a pediatric nurse. How can I help?" Our need had been supplied!

I could share time after time when God's split-second timing was perfect. The roads we've traveled have led us on journeys that have solidified my faith, many involving times when we had mechanical troubles. One Sunday afternoon we loaded up after an early concert to head down the road to the evening service at another church when we realized our bus wasn't running right. Brian and I looked at each other and breathed a prayer. When the pastor found out about our difficulty, he came back in a few minutes with a mechanic who had been in the service that morning. Although the mechanic had not intended to be in church that day, the Lord had directed him to our need. Soon we were rolling down the road again. We love our "fringe benefits"—life insurance that never fails!

Our music ministry is extremely diverse. On one Sunday we may minister in a church of 4,000, and then the next Sunday we may find ourselves in a tiny country church. Many times we'll minister in churches that are unable to meet our financial needs. But the Lord always provides for us. It's not unusual to come home from such a trip to find a check in the mail with a note that says, "God put you on our hearts. Please accept this gift." That's how we're able to persevere.

Over the years the Lord has confirmed our faith through His care for us. He always gives me just what I need to support Brian and the boys as we serve God together. So when someone asks about my "job," I always answer that I'm so glad God trusted me enough to send His "help wanted ad" to me. And I'm so glad my answer was yes!

PENNI ARNER WORKS WITH HER HUSBAND, BRIAN, IN BRIAN ARNER MINISTRIES. PENNI TRAVELS WITH BRIAN AND THEIR SONS SPREADING THE GOSPEL THROUGH MUSIC. THEY RESIDE IN CUMMING, GEORGIA, WHEN NOT ON THE ROAD.

JOYCE WILLIAMS
HIS EYE IS ON *THIS* SPARROW

God had been faithful to provide a new job in ministry, a new home, and now . . .

Reality was setting in. I had given my notice at the office. Boxes were stacked in most rooms of my house, and sorting 26 years of memories was underway. It was a bittersweet time of saying yes to God's tomorrows and good-bye to yesterdays. I kept thinking, *How can I leave my family? They need me—I need them!* It certainly was a good thing that God had already healed me from my fears and had given me unshakable faith!

When I left Clearwater on that second visit, Pastor Mark had thrust a videotape into my hands. It was a copy of a live taping of a Talleys/Kingsmen concert that had been recorded at the church. I loved it. A young local singer named Brian Arner, the introductory artist for the concert, sang a couple of songs, one of which was "His Eye Is on the Sparrow." As I sat on the floor packing and saying goodbye to many memories, I found myself replaying that song over and over. It was just the reassurance I needed. Months later I told Brian that his song "got me out of town."

What a whirlwind! Finishing up at the office; saying goodbye to family, friends, and all things familiar; packing—it was all a blur. Finally, on Thanksgiving Day my family met for an early dinner. I glimpsed glints of tears in their eyes—or were they just a reflection of my own? Then I got into the car. I could hardly take my eyes off my loved ones framed in my nephew's front door. I'm sure they felt somewhat skeptical about what I was doing—why I was leaving. But they did not discourage me. I kept turning back to wave goodbye. Then my Himalyan cat, Snickers, and I headed south in my packed-to-the-hilt Buick.

I'll never forget my arrival in Clearwater. Arrangements had been made for me to live in a mobile home park for a couple of weeks until I could close on my condominium and complete the renovations. What a sight I must have been un-loading that car—a middle-aged woman and her cat—but they let me stay!

Those first weeks were very intense. It was a totally differ-ent assignment for me, for Pastor Mark, and for the church. Everybody probably wondered what I was doing—including me! But the presence of the Lord was very real.

I missed my family, and that was the hardest part. My daughter Tami came to Clearwater for Christmas break from college, and she fell in love with the beaches and palm trees. I remember that first Saturday morning as we ate breakfast right on Clearwater Beach. We looked at each other, and I said, "We're not on vacation—I live here!" As a matter of fact, Tami was so enamored with Clearwater that she decided to stay and finish her last few college credits locally. So God brought my daughter to live with me before I had been there a month! She and I even got to drive to North Carolina to have Christmas with my other daughter, Beth, and her hus-band at Aunt Jo's and Uncle Rob's place. It made our first holiday much easier.

It was wonderful to watch the Lord do great things. As minister of Christian education and outreach, my assignment was to motivate the people of the church to find their areas of spiritual giftedness and to get involved. It was a joy to see the church move into high gear! Wednesday nights became ministry opportunities, and many members soon had an area of responsibility. The excitement and enthusiasm that developed was delightful to see. The greatest blessing of all was to see new people being won to the Lord.

It amazed me to see what God was doing through that ministry. That He would use me—a thrown-away sparrow—to be a little part of it was extraordinary. As the inimitable Ethel Waters used to say after singing "His Eye Is on the Sparrow"—"And He watches over us birds too!"

I'm so glad His eye was on me!

Dana Roberts

DO SOMETHING ABOUT ME!

*M*om, is there a God and a heaven and a hell?" I asked.

"Oh, don't worry about that," she replied. "Nobody ever talks about it."

And she was right. At least not in my family—except when used in a profane way. But still, I couldn't get the question out of my mind. When Aunt Margie came to eat supper with us, she prayed to Him before she ate. Not only that, but the rest of us were expected to shut our mouths and bow our heads while she did it! Aunt Margie seemed to respect and even love the God she prayed to. Why? What did He ever do for her? And if He was real, what did He ever do for me? Nothing!

In fact, the more I thought about it, the angrier I became. If this God was so good, why did Mom's boyfriend come into my room in the middle of the night? Why did He allow Mom to ignore Daddy's abuse of my sister and me? Why did He let Daddy beat Mom until she bled? If this God was so good, why didn't He keep me safe? If this God was so good, why did I feel so ashamed and dirty and scared?

A few years later, I came to a conclusion. I was going to issue a challenge to God! I stood in the middle of my bedroom, looked up at the ceiling with clenched fists and teeth, and said contemptuously, *If You're such a big, bad, powerful God, do something about me!*

When I drank so much Seagram's Seven or Jack Daniels

that I couldn't remember what I had done or with whom, sometimes I thought, *Didn't stop me, did You, God?* When I decided to "go stealing" and left the store with the merchandise, I thought, *Some powerful God You are!* and laughed. And when the stress really started to get to me, I smoked a joint or two and thought, *I'm not hurting anybody, I just need to calm down.* Shaky times.

And then the slightest little thought came to me like a leaf that slowly falls and lands precariously on a ledge: *Am I hurting anybody?* Who was it that was making me wonder if what I was doing mattered? Why was it that, even though everyone I knew was heartily in favor of a wild lifestyle, I was beginning to wonder if I was still in favor of it?

And then it happened—God met my challenge.

One night while I was lying in my bed, He gave me the full realization that the choices I was making hurt *Him*. As the tears began to flow, I got out of bed, got onto my knees, and said, *God, I don't know anything about You really, but I do know that the things I'm doing are wrong, and I know that if You don't help me, I'm a lost cause. I need You to help me make it through this. Come into my life and help me.* At last a weight lifted from me.

Since then, God has revealed some amazing truths to me. Even before I knew He was "doing something about me," He was. He was giving me faith before I even recognized it. He didn't stop me from drinking or having premarital sex or stealing or experimenting with drugs or any of the other self-destructive things I was doing. He did, however, make me understand that it was He who kept me from being killed when I drove drunk the wrong way on a one-way street. It was He who kept me from getting pregnant, contracting a venereal disease, or being thrown in jail. Why? He was "doing something about me"—but what?

He was loving me to himself. He was growing my faith for the shaky times to come. And there would be plenty. I realized that if God was big enough, powerful enough, and loving enough to call me to himself in the midst of my rebellion, He certainly would continue to love, guide, and extend mercy to me while I was trying to figure out how He wanted me to live.

Through those lessons, God has blessed me in many ways. In my most turbulent times He sent a handsome, quiet-spoken, Christian young man into my life who later became my husband. Kevin gives me small glimpses of what God must be like. Through my dear husband God also gave me a godly family who loves and supports me completely. He has given me a second chance at childhood through our two daughters, Haley and Olivia. And for all the tears I cried in the desert of my youth, I now have life—and life abundant to His glory!

I am filled with a joy that comes from the answered, angry prayer of a 12-year-old and a life lived walking with the God who is the Master Faith-Stretcher!

DANA ROBERTS IS A VIBRANT COMMUNICATOR AND BIBLE TEACHER WHO IS ACTIVE IN BIBLE STUDY FELLOWSHIP. SHE AND HER HUSBAND, KEVIN, ARE THE PARENTS OF TWO DAUGHTERS AND RESIDE IN THE WOODLANDS, TEXAS.

JESSICA PLEASANT
BE FRUITFUL AND MULTIPLY

When I think back on the dysfunction of the blended family in which I grew up in Lake City, South Carolina, I should have expected a shipwreck. But one spring day in 1985 when I gave my heart to the Lord, my life changed. I began to dream of better days. I could picture a long dining room table with my handsome husband sitting at one end and my many children lining the sides between us laughing and calling, "Mommy, please pass the peas."

The handsome man of my dreams came into my life, and Reggie and I were married on December 5, 1987. We shared a desire for lots of children, so six months into our marriage we were off and running in our attempt to be fruitful and multiply.

After a year of trying to conceive and a miscarriage, our doctor explained that our complications indicated infertility. More specifically, they pointed to me. My newly found faith plummeted, and my dining room table vision began to fade. After enduring years of unsuccessful pregnancies, I finally acknowledged that I did not have the strength to continue. Only my faith in God kept me going.

Somehow God helped me as I faced disappointments, surgeries, and procedures that were accompanied by overwhelming anxiety and tears. My faith was shaky, but it never collapsed. He always stabilized me even when I was wavering.

During those long days and nights He unfailingly gave me exactly what it took to hold me steady. He hushed my restless soul as He sang His word to me like a mother singing lullabies over her child. Time after time, in the midst of such anguish, I felt His comforting touch.

Can you imagine our excitement the day I found out I was pregnant? This time our prayers were answered. After years of barrenness, God gave us our darling son, Joshua. Then He added another beautiful blessing—our precious daughter, Sarah.

Those years of despair taught me more than I ever would have learned from the houseful of kids I dreamed of. I learned that the foundation of my faith is the solid rock of Jesus Christ. By anchoring tight to His promises, I could make it through whatever comes across my path.

I asked over and over to be a fruitful, multiplying wife and mother. God gave me that desire of my heart. The bonus is that He also enabled me to become a woman of faith who is bearing fruit and multiplying each day. As my husband ministers to the players on the Tennessee Titans National Football League team, I have the privilege of ministering to their wives. Very few people understand the pressures that professional football players and their families experience. Reggie and I understand because of the years he played.

God is helping me share the faith that held me steady through those years. I can testify to others of an unshakable faith that will keep them, too, steady during their shaky times.

JESSICA PLEASANT AND HER HUSBAND, REGGIE, ARE FULL-TIME MISSIONARIES ON STAFF WITH CAMPUS CRUSADE FOR CHRIST UNDER THE DIVISIONAL MINISTRY OF ATHLETES-IN-ACTION, AND REGGIE SERVES AS CHAPLAIN OF THE TENNESSEE TITANS PROFESSIONAL FOOTBALL TEAM. THEY ARE THE PARENTS OF JOSHUA AND SARAH AND RESIDE IN BRENTWOOD, TENNESSEE.

JOYCE WILLIAMS
HEART'S DESIRE

$\mathcal{T}$he Lord was doing great things in my life and in my new ministry. The gracious people at Clearwater First Church of the Nazarene were extraordinarily kind and patient with me. We learned a lot together about growing ministry, and Pastor Mark and Vanessa were delightful. It was such fun to take part in grandma-like activities. I even got to see their son, Josh, turn over for the first time.

The Lord blessed, and new people kept coming. Many in the congregation were involved as never before—making phone calls, delivering pies to visitors, writing letters, praying for those going out to present the gospel, discipling new believers, and on and on. It was a wonderful team effort, and we had a great time.

In March our church sponsored a mission trip to Puerto Rico to build a parsonage for the young pastor and his wife in Loquillo. I had received notice the previous week from the attorney that the divorce would be finalized the week we were away. The finality of that—the fact that I was really going to be a divorced person—was very difficult for me.

We had a wonderful week of working and witnessing in the town. It was a blessing to lead some of the local people to the Lord. Each night as I collapsed into my sleeping bag on the floor, though, I thought, *Divorced! When I get back I'll really be divorced!* And I wept quietly into my flimsy pillow.

When our work in Loquillo was completed, we said a tear-ful good-bye to our new friends and boarded the van for San Juan. We walked through the streets of that picturesque city. When we got to the ancient fort, I told the group that I was going to take a little time on the beach by myself. As I walked down the time-worn steps, I felt very close to my Heavenly Husband.

Oblivious to the breathtaking panorama of white beach, azure seas, and brilliant skies stretched out before me, I could think only of the fact that I was now divorced. I felt as if I had a scarlet letter dangling from a chain around my neck. I mourned the death of my marriage and grieved for the family that had been splintered.

An inveterate beach scavenger, I paused to pick up fragments of shells and other items strewn across the sandy expanses. I dropped them into my pocket beside my small New Testament with Psalms. Reflectively, I praised God for the miraculous doors that had been opened to me. Ps. 37:4 came to me, and I repeated it out loud: "Delight yourself in the LORD, and He will give you the desires of your heart." God had been so faithful to me. His presence surrounded me, and I was filled with renewed hope and peace as I stood there in His open-air, sandy cathedral.

I cried out, *Husband, Father, God—I'm really hurting today. Could you please give me something tangible to hold onto—a reminder of Your love?* I paused, reflecting on the verse about our heart's desires. Then I added, *It would mean so much to me if I could find something heart-shaped.* A large, flat rock on the edge of the crashing waves caught my eye, and I walked out to it. Clambering up the sides, I found it to be a perfect pew in that watery sanctuary. And my Heavenly Husband whispered to my soul.

As we communed, I gazed around me at the beauty of my surroundings. I began to hum an old song, "The Love of

God," and it seemed as though I could almost hear the words
accompanied by the cacophonic background of ocean noises.
I caught my breath as my lips mouthed the words of the second verse. My eyes filled with tears of joy, and I softly sang,

> *Could we with ink the ocean fill,*
> *And were the sky of parchment made,*
> *Were ev'ry stalk on earth a quill,*
> *And ev'ry man a scribe by trade,*
> *To write the love of God above*
> *Would drain the ocean dry;*
> *Nor could the scroll contain the whole,*
> *Tho' stretched from sky to sky.*

Joyously, I began to sing out loud,

> *O love of God, how rich and pure!*
> *How measureless and strong!*
> *It shall forevermore endure—*
> *The saints' and angels' song!*
> —Frederick M. Lehman

My heart swelled with an overwhelming knowledge of
God's love. I sat there in that sun-splashed spot looking out at
the glistening turquoise ocean. It seemed that I could still
hear echoes of the strains of God's love song as the waves
roared and crashed onto the shore. The last of my despair fell
away as I looked out at the vast Atlantic stretching as far as I
could see, draped with the canopy of crystal blue skies. I tried
to imagine countless hands dipping quill pens into that im-
mense ocean. The futility of any attempt to transcribe the im-
mensity of God's love onto seemingly infinite parchment
skies was obvious. That reality permeated my being, and I
could almost hear an angelic chorus echoing that beautiful
song.

Then I heard a faint whisper in my soul. My Heavenly
Husband told me, *Someday you'll stand on this shore with the*

man I'll give to you. He'll share your heart for ministry and your love for Me.

It seemed as though I had spent hours on that rock in sweet communion with God. Alarmed, I looked at my watch and saw that it was time to rejoin my group. Quickly, I picked up my sandals and hurried across the beach to climb back up to the fort. As I walked, I prayed, *Father, forgive me for asking for a special memento. Thank You for this blessed serendipity in the sand.*

When I got to the fort's courtyard, I sat down on a bench, dusted the sand from my feet, and put on my sandals. Then I decided to quickly examine the items I had picked up on the beach when I first started walking. Incredibly, right in the middle of an assortment of shells and other relics was a lilac-colored, *heart-shaped* stone! Imagine my delight. My Heavenly Husband had delivered my heart's desire even before I asked for it. I was filled with an all-consuming presence of divine love.

As I walked back to my group, I felt as if I was returning from another planet. My experience was too fresh and special to share with anyone right then, but as we rode in the van to the home of Pedro Cruz, the superintendent of the Puerto Rico District, for dinner, I asked the others if they could help me remember all of the lyrics of "The Love of God," and I quickly scribbled them down. Someone reminded me that Rev. Cruz has a beautiful voice. When we got to his house I asked him to sing that song for us, and he graciously consented. My heart was stirred as he sang it first in English and then in Spanish. Once more I was filled with an awesome and amazing love beyond expression.

That evening as we flew back home, I clutched my little "heart" in my hand, rubbing it in wonder. The next afternoon I showed it to Tami and told her what had happened on the beach. On Monday I repeated the story to my dear friend Lee, minister of music at Clearwater First Church.

Later that day as I was returning to my office at the church, I slipped a brand-new Dallas Holm tape into my car's player. I could hardly believe it when he began to sing none other than "The Love of God." In that particular rendition I could hear the roaring of the ocean and the crashing waves just as I had heard them beating upon the shores of the beach in San Juan. When I got back to the church I ran to the music room to find Lee. I cried, "My Heavenly Husband sent a love song to me!" And I played the tape for her.

In her inimitable way she responded, "The next thing you'll be telling me is that He's sent flowers to you!"

And He did! Imagine my delighted surprise the next morning to find that a lily that had practically died in my move to Clearwater months before had two beautiful, snow-white blooms bursting from it! I could hardly wait to get to church to tell Lee that He had indeed sent flowers.

A few days later a neighbor knocked on my door to invite me to go shopping. While she was in a store I decided to go into the jewelry shop next door. I showed my "heart" to the jeweler, and he looked at it under magnification. I believed it was a fragment of glass that had been weathered by the sun, sand, and tides. But he immediately informed me that it was not glass—no bubbles were present. After I told him my story, he insisted that I take it to a gemologist but made me promise to return to let him know what I discovered.

Later that week I walked into another jewelry shop at the mall. After the gemologist looked at my little heart-shaped stone, he asked, "Where did you get this?" I told him my story, and then he responded, "What you have is a moonstone." He told me that moonstones are part of the topaz family. When I told him I had found it in Puerto Rico, he was amazed. On my way home I remembered reading about the foundations of heaven in Rev. 21. Later that evening tears filled my eyes as I read in verse 20 that the ninth layer of the city walls foundation is topaz. What a precious treasure!

When I returned to the first jeweler as he had requested, he mounted my lilac heart in a lovely gold setting and attached it to a chain to wear over my heart. I found myself constantly touching it and was always deeply comforted. I understood in a new way the meaning of David's words. Truly, God gives us our heart's desires. And He alone truly knows our hearts because He made them!

KIM SINGSON
THE WORK MUST GO ON

*A*s I sat in anguish by the bedside of my beloved husband who lay dying of cancer, my heart ached with loss and grief as I contemplated life without this dear man. We had been such a team—working together for the Lord. Our children and I would miss him immeasurably. How could I go on without him? Cushioned by memories, I reflected on the past during those lonely night hours.

I had been so blessed to grow up in a Christian home, and I accepted Jesus as my Savior when I was nine years old. From that day there had never been any doubt that I had made a lifetime commitment to serve the Lord. After graduating from a Christian high school, I went on to study at the university. The Lord impressed me to organize the Ladies' Gospel Team, and we visited a number of churches in the hills of Manipur sharing the good news of Jesus Christ.

It was a great day when I met a young preacher named T. S. Singson, the principal of Christian Special Boarding School, where I began to teach. He gathered with several of us for special times of prayer and became the founding chairman of the Youth Prayer Fellowship. As we gathered for all-night prayer meetings, we began to see wonderful answers that came as a result of those prayer times.

T. S. and I fell in love and were married in January 1979. We continued to teach at the school for two years. It was our greatest joy to share Jesus with the students as we provided secular and spiritual education. With great joy we welcomed our first child, Jenny, into our lives in 1980 and dedicated her to His service.

Upon completion of my bachelor of arts degree in 1981, I organized a Women's Bible Camp, the first ever to be held in Manipur. A year later we moved to Pune, India, to study at Union Biblical Seminary. Those were very difficult years, and we had very little money. But God always sustained and provided for us. As I studied, my vision and burden for my people intensified. Jenny prayed for a little brother, and Samuel was born in our final year of studies in answer to her prayers.

In 1993 we completed our master's degrees, and in 1994 we joined the Church of the Nazarene. My husband was appointed to be the first coordinator for the work in Manipur, and it was a joy to return to our home area. We worked together writing and translating, preaching and teaching. They were very busy and challenging years, but we enjoyed sharing the good news of Jesus Christ. Our son, Daniel, was born in 1994.

I was ordained in January 2001. However, my joy was overshadowed when we got word that my dear husband had cancer. We were stunned to get that diagnosis, and we prayed intensely for his healing. Three months later I found myself sitting by his deathbed wondering how I could go on. With three children and my sister's orphaned daughter in my care, there were times when I felt overwhelmed.

But as T. S. and I shared those last days, we both knew that God's will was for the work to go on. Even though the walls around my life were crumbling, I knew that God would get me through this heartbreaking time. Just as I had preached and taught for years, I knew the Lord would give me the guidance, strength, and courage I would need. And that's just what He did. Although it hasn't been easy, He has provided everything

I've needed. Since my husband's death, my life has become even busier in carrying on the work of the kingdom.

Although it's very unusual in our culture, I was privileged to be appointed as my husband's successor as coordinator to carry on our work with the churches in Manipur. I'm also a *JESUS* film coach and church planter. In addition, I'm involved in translating books and literature from English to our dialect, Thadou-Kuki. Every Saturday we conduct prayer and fasting in all of our churches throughout Manipur. It is a special blessing to see so many involved, especially the young people. I travel extensively to different parts of India teaching, training, and sharing the gospel. All our children are serving the Lord and are involved in the work of the Kingdom. I can verify that unshakable faith in God will keep us strong even when the world around us seems to crumble.

The responsibility is quite heavy, and the work is very intense. I must rely on the Lord's strength constantly. He who has called me is faithful, and He enables me to carry on. His work must go forward, and I know He'll be with me until I complete my task.

KIM SINGSON IS THE COORDINATOR OF 17 CHURCHES SCATTERED THROUGHOUT THE MANIPUR AREA OF INDIA. SHE IS A *JESUS* FILM COACH AND CHURCH PLANTER. SHE RESIDES IN CHURACHANDPUR, INDIA.

SELVI MARY DINAKARAN

DON'T KILL MY HUSBAND!

I've discovered that being the wife of a pastor/evangelist brings both joy and pain. Sometimes both of us pay a high price. One of those times was during a Sunday service in 1984. It was one of the worst days of my life.

I had married my pastor, Solomon Dinakaran, a year before that day and was nine months pregnant with our first child. Our whole church had gathered in the village of Chennasandra to celebrate the conversion of Mr. Subramani. As an alcoholic, he had been a notorious thug in his village and was a nuisance to society. My husband shared the gospel with Mr. Subramani, and he and his family accepted Jesus as their personal Savior. He changed his name to Samuel and was baptized. Fifty of us gathered to start a new church in his home and to sing praises to the Lord. As we sang, we began to hear a great commotion outside.

To our dismay we discovered that a mob of more than 100 people had gathered in front of the house. Raviraj Samy, the Communist leader in that area, was their leader. They ordered my husband to come out of the house. As he stepped out of the front door with a smile, they began beating him mercilessly. Raviraj Samy hit him with a heavy blow in the face, and his mouth started bleeding profusely. I pushed my way outside screaming, "Don't kill my husband!" But they paid no attention to me as they screamed, cursed, and beat him. They yelled, "Why are you preaching Jesus here? Why are you trying to change this into a Christian village? We won't tolerate you—we'll kill you! Stop trying to change our people! No more prayer in this village! Today is the final day for you!" And they continued to beat Solomon.

I cried and screamed as I watched the blood stream down his face, and I began to feel pains in my stomach. Our congregation gathered around me. Solomon caught my eye and said, "Don't cry. I'll be all right." He said to our people, "Don't retaliate. Everything will work out." Then he asked his attackers if he could tell them something, and my husband shared with them about Jesus. (Later he said it was the best sermon he ever preached because he thought it might be his last one!) He was calm and ready to face anything for the sake of the gospel of Jesus Christ—even death. All I could think of was that I was going to lose my husband and maybe my baby. My heart hurt and tears streamed down my face as our people and I prayed for God to deliver us.

Miraculously, our prayers were answered. The police came and began to break up the crowd. They saw my distress and rescued my husband from the angry mob. I was so relieved and glad that my husband was spared. It was my first experience with persecution, but somehow I knew it was not going to be my last. Raviraj Samy was very angry when he and the mob left. Because of God's answer I felt peace, and the events of that day became a great witness to the entire village.

Solomon said, "Don't worry. God will take care of us. We must pray for the salvation of the people who attacked me." He said, "While Raviraj Samy was beating me, God showed me that if he can motivate 100 people to attack me, think of what he could do for the Kingdom!" So we began to pray for all of them. A few days later our daughter was born safely.

Three months afterwards Raviraj Samy crushed his hand in an accident—the same hand that had pummeled Solomon. People began to say, "This happened because he beat that Christian pastor." I'm not sure of that. But I do know that a number of people in Chennasandra became Christians as a result.

Raviraj Samy became very depressed. Our church continued to pray for him. One day in deep despair (actually he was under conviction), he decided to go out into the forest to hang himself. As he prepared to loop a rope around a tree limb, he looked on the ground. There was a piece of paper that said, "Jesus loves you." He thought, *Jesus is that pastor's God! I must go to see him.*

He ran home, got his family together, and they came to our house. When I saw him at the door, I thought, *He's come back to kill us this time!* But instead, he said, "I want to know your God." He and his family were saved that day. They stayed for hours. After a while Raviraj Samy said, "I believe that God wants me to be a preacher like you."

Solomon said, "I agree with you. I've known that since the day you beat me." Then he pulled out an envelope stuffed with money he had been saving for this reason. He said, "This is the money you'll need to go to Bible school to study to be a pastor." Within just a few weeks he and his family moved to the Bible school. He became a great pastor and planted many churches.

Every drop of blood that my husband shed has become the seed for planting another church in that area. It's true that "Those who sow in tears will reap with joy" (Ps. 126:5).

SELVI MARY DINAKARAN IS A SPEAKER AND AN ORDAINED ELDER IN THE CHURCH OF THE NAZARENE. SHE LIVES IN WHITEFIELD, INDIA, WITH HER HUSBAND, SOLOMON, WHO IS THE DISTRICT SUPERINTENDENT OF TWO DISTRICTS. ALL THREE OF THEIR CHILDREN HAVE BEEN CALLED TO FULL-TIME CHRISTIAN SERVICE.

JOYCE WILLIAMS

PRINCE CHARMING—
THE LAND OF OZ

On the beach in San Juan, my Heavenly Husband had promised He would send me a man who would share my heart for ministry and my love for God.

The Lord began to open other doors of opportunity. I enjoyed speaking at a retreat for the wonderful people from a church south of Miami. We had a great time in the Lord, and afterward I stood out on the dock with Chloe, the director, and we shared for a long time. As we were leaving, she said, "You should meet my former pastor, Gene Williams. He lost his dear wife, Bettye, in January. You'd make a great couple. He pastors a church out in Kansas." As Chloe continued, I agreed that he sounded like a great man of God.

Life was good. I loved what I was doing and was extremely busy. Later that year, Lee also mentioned Gene Williams to me. Brian Arner and his wife, Penni, were members of our church at Clearwater. Brian travels and sings all over the continent and had sung at Wichita First Church, where Gene pastored. They thought he had practically hung the moon.

My dear friend who first mentioned Clearwater First Church to me, Nina Gunter, came to Clearwater to speak for our Faith Promise Convention. She used a scripture that has become a foundational promise for my life—Habakkuk 1:5, which reads, "I am going to do something in your days that you would not believe, even if you were told." I claimed that promise. My faith was soaring!

The months rolled by. God was blessing, and my life was fulfilled as never before. My Heavenly Husband was divine and provided every need. About a year after I stood on the dock with Chloe and heard about that Kansas pastor, Brian Arner came into my office at church. I had asked him questions about Gene from time to time. That day I asked, "When are you scheduled to sing at Wichita First?"

He opened his calendar and said, "This fall."

I said, "Are you going to be talking to him anytime soon?"

He said, "Yes. I may call him today."

Then I said, "You can tell him about me if you think that would be appropriate. He sounds like a great man."

Brian called that afternoon and told me that he had called Wichita First. Then he said, "Pastor Williams would like to call you. But he wants a picture." A picture! Did he have a photo album of prospects? Oh, well—I had nothing to lose. So I took an older picture to Brian, who mailed it to Wichita.

Gene called about a week later, but the first couple of times he called I was out of the office. When we finally talked for the first time, it was amazing. It was as if we had known each other for years. He began to call frequently and then every day. We found that we had a great deal in common. Pretty soon he was calling several times each day.

Gene flew down to meet me in April 1992, and it was pretty much a "done deal." I began to believe that this godly man was the one for me. He flew me to Wichita the next month, and I met his great family and the wonderful people at church. (I sure am glad that God had already healed me of fear!) Although I was a divorced woman and that was not an ideal agenda for a pastor's wife, he proposed, and I accepted. I was headed toward "the Land of Oz"!

I'll never forget our first visit to Roanoke to introduce Gene to my family. Uncle Lewis was our family's surviving patriarch. When Gene asked for his blessing on our marriage, Uncle Lewis hesitated a little. He knew what I had been through and was somewhat protective. When Gene went into the other room, Uncle Lewis said, "Seems like a nice fellow. I just hope he's the Prince Charming you think he is." I guess that was his blessing.

On the way to the Wichita church on September 21, 1992, tears of joy spilled out of my eyes. Later, as I stood at the back of the chapel listening to Steve Betts play "The Love of God," I remembered that day on the beach in San Juan. Rain pelted the roof of the chapel and thunder rumbled, and I was reminded of the waves pounding that shore in San Juan. I touched my heart pendant and thanked God for this new life, for the unwavering faith He had instilled within me.

And, yes, Uncle Lewis—after more than a decade with me, Gene is still my Prince Charming extraordinaire!

VONETTE BRIGHT
BELIEVING GOD FOR
THE IMPOSSIBLE

*B*ill, you have pulmonary fibrosis. It's worse than cancer. It's worse than heart disease. It's worse than just about anything, because there is no cure." Dr. Willis spoke very seriously, because Bill seemed not to recognize just how ill he was.

Believing God for the impossible is not new to Bill Bright. It's true that he's always been so absorbed in doing the Lord's work that he depends almost solely on God to take care of all health needs. He complied with most of the doctor's directions but was continuing to meet his scheduled commitments. His reaction to the doctor's news was "Praise the Lord—I'll go to see Jesus soon!"

How did I, as a wife, react to such news? We had thought we were doing the right things by watching our diet, exercising, and taking the prescribed medications. We thought we were being very health conscious.

Pulmonary fibrosis was at first only a suggested diagnosis, and we endeavored to have it confirmed at Mayo Clinic in Jacksonville. We both had medical exams at the same time. Our consultation times conflicted, so neither of us heard the final report of the other. That was a mistake I made by not realizing that my positive-minded husband was prone to focus only on the positive. As far as he was concerned, it was not a definite diagnosis.

At the suggestion of our local pulmonologist, several

months later we went to Mayo Clinic in Rochester, Minnesota. There we were told that only a lung biopsy could provide a conclusive diagnosis.

The doctors at Mayo helped us squarely face the fact that we were in deep water healthwise. We went to our knees with a new realization that only a supernatural act of God was going to meet this need in our lives. As we prayed, we remembered that we had found God faithful in dramatic ways for years. This would be a new adventure in faith. Perhaps God would allow a cure to be found for this disease and that not only Bill but also others would be healed. We and others around the world were praying for Bill. It would be just like the Lord to perform a miracle.

We praised God for our marriage of more than 50 years, our ministry, our precious family, and the blessed association with Campus Crusade for Christ staff and friends. We believed that to do anything less than praise Him in the midst of this difficult stage of our lives would be ingratitude and an insult to our Heavenly Father. Praise the Lord—everything that happens to His children is filtered through His love.

We made our need for prayer public. The biopsy was done in Denver to confirm the diagnosis. We reiterated in our request for prayer that there is no cure. We want to be certain that if God chooses to heal Bill, it will be He who receives the glory.

Bill's medical team has been fabulous. We're leaving no stone unturned as we walk by faith with our hands securely in the hand of Jesus. He has answered our prayers by allowing Bill to live to celebrate 50 years of ministry, to see the installation of Steve Douglass, his successor in ministry, and to celebrate Bill's 80th birthday. He has completed eight books, and six more books will be complete soon. He has also launched a new ministry within Campus Crusade, the Pastors' Global

Network. He is not healed, but right now he is enjoying a better quality of life than one year ago, and we continue to trust the Lord.

God has used many passages of scripture to minister to me and to encourage my heart during the last two years. One is Ps. 57. One of the key verses in this passage is verse 7—"My heart is confident in you, O God; no wonder I can sing your praises!" (NLT).

Bill and I continue to rejoice in God's goodness and believe Him for the impossible.

SINCE COFOUNDING CAMPUS CRUSADE FOR CHRIST WITH HER HUSBAND, BILL, IN 1951, VONETTE BRIGHT HAS MAINTAINED A RIGOROUS SCHEDULE AS HOSTESS, EVANGELIST, DISCIPLER, AND AUTHOR OF MANY BOOKS. AS FOUNDER OF WOMEN TODAY INTERNATIONAL, SHE IS WIDELY RECOGNIZED AS A SPOKESPERSON FOR CHRISTIAN WOMEN. SHE AND BILL HAVE TWO SONS AND RESIDE IN ORLANDO, FLORIDA.

FAYE SPEER

THROUGH IT ALL

wo things I have learned in life are that God never fails and that we all go through changes. I am blessed to have been born into a Christian home. My father was a minister, so I learned many lessons about faith and about living from him and my mother. My parents provided the foundation for my life by teaching me about loving the Lord, the importance of family, hard work, sacrifice, honesty, patience in waiting on the Lord, and trusting Him for all I need.

A big change in my life came when I went to a Christian boarding high school in Nashville. I loved being with other young people of the same faith. But I certainly wasn't prepared to be responsible for doing my laundry and taking care of all of the things my mother had always done for me. Soldiers were coming home from World War II. When I first laid eyes on Brock Speer, I knew he was the one for me. We fell in love and were married—then my life really shifted into high gear!

As pioneers of southern gospel music, The Speers sang all over the country. I traveled and sang with the group until our three children started coming. Then I stayed home with them for the most part. It seemed that no emergency ever happened until Daddy left. I recall some dark days while trying to take care of the things that men usually do. Sometimes my faith was stretched as I had to learn about getting the house roofed, calling the plumber, getting a new water heater, hiring painters, calling the right repairmen when the heat went off, and shoveling snow. With God's help, I always made it.

On Sundays I would get all three kids ready and head to church. If it was raining or snowing, I would hand the kids off to a greeter and go park the car. Brock always told me I could take care of anything but trading cars. Somehow my faith didn't stretch that far. But in the past few years since he passed away, I've had to do just that. I can imagine him saying to me now, "I just knew you would do that someday!" It's amazing how our faith grows through necessity.

After the children were gone, I started traveling with Brock and the group full-time. Many people think that traveling on a bus is an exciting way of life. That's because they don't hear much about the all-night drives as you chase your bed while the bus climbs curvy mountain roads followed by trying to look decent for Sunday morning's concert. Every morning when I got up, Brock would have the coffee ready. We would hunt for the church restroom hoping for warm water with which to wash our hair and freshen up a bit. Washing my hair in cold water is not one of my favorite things, but it sure wakes you up! Now that I'm home, I thank God every Sunday morning for a good warm shower!

So many funny things happened along the way. One Sunday morning I was wearing a beautiful beige-and-white suit, and I thought I looked pretty good. As we sat down for the pastor to take the offering, Karen, who was singing with us, asked me to go to the restroom with her. As soon as we got there, she bent over laughing—two inches of my slip was showing. I promptly took it off and stuffed it into a planter. I'm sure the people wondered what had happened to the lace when I went back out onto the platform! I'm just glad nobody found it in the planter—and that I remembered to sneak it out and take it with me after the service.

Another evening we were singing in a church that had rather dark carpet. As I was leaving the platform, I didn't see the step, and down I went. It happened to be behind the organ, so people in the congregation said I just seemed to disappear. Members of the choir later told me that I fell very gracefully with my skirt spread around me. Talk about embarrassing moments!

Our faith was tested many times, such as with problems with the bus and with staying in close touch with the family while we were on the road. Regardless of what came across our path and where our journeys took us, God was always with us and supplied just what we needed. Our faith was secure even on the shakiest rides.

Through all these years, God has been with me every step of the way. He saw me through breast cancer. Then there were the years when Brock was sick and we had to leave the road. Just months before he went to be with Jesus, we celebrated our 50th wedding anniversary.

The Lord has continued to give me the grace and the faith I need. I never really understood about the peace that passes all understanding until I had to deal with Brock's death. Oh, yes—pain, loneliness, and hurt remain with me. But my faith holds steady because I believe in the One who has control of my life.

Through it all, I've learned to trust more completely in Jesus and His precious Word.

FAYE SPEER AND HER LATE HUSBAND, BROCK, TRAVELED MANY YEARS SINGING WITH THE SPEERS. HER WARM HEART AND TENDER SPIRIT ALONG WITH HER RICH CONTRALTO VOICE HAVE CAPTURED HEARTS AROUND THE WORLD. FAYE HAS THREE CHILDREN AND RESIDES IN NASHVILLE.

MARY THOMPSON
WALKING BY FAITH

On a November night in 1988 my life was changed forever. My husband, Charles, and I were on our way home from a church meeting. At 8:15 a car traveling more than 60 miles per hour crossed the grassy median and hit us head-on. Almost simultaneously, another car plowed into us from behind, crushing our vehicle like an accordion. Minutes later as the rescue teams arrived on the scene, they shook their heads and said, "No way anybody could have survived this one." But they found four of us alive—both of the other drivers, Charles, and me. The other drivers were not hurt badly since, ironically, both had been drinking. But Charles and I clung to life by a thread.

I was conscious as the rescue team worked for more than an hour to free us. The pain was excruciating, but my greatest fear was Charles' silence. As I lay there crushed and bleeding, unable to reach out to Charles, I cried and prayed.

Soon after we were rushed to the Medical College of Virginia in Richmond, word began to spread, and prayers bombarded heaven on our behalf. We needed every one of them. Charles had suffered a severely depressed skull fracture, a broken jaw, and his right arm was broken in three places. He also sustained broken ribs, a collapsed lung, and several lacerations to his head and face. He was in intensive care, unconscious, and listed in critical condition. He wasn't expected to survive the night.

I had broken ribs, multiple internal injuries requiring surgery, and extensive damage to both of my feet and ankles. My feet had been crushed by the impact, and my left foot was almost severed. The injuries were equivalent to what I would have sustained if I had jumped from a five-story building and landed directly on my feet.

Charles and I were on different floors, and I could hardly stand not being able to see him. He was unconscious and remained in a coma for five weeks, during which he underwent several bouts of infection, including pneumonia and meningitis. There were days when the doctors were certain he would not make it, but my faith remained strong. Although the surgeries and intense pain were sometimes almost more than I could bear, I knew the Lord would get us through. He always had.

When the doctor told us that Charles's brain had been bruised but not punctured, we were encouraged. But a prognosis for full recovery without brain damage was extremely uncertain. I was told that it was very unlikely I would ever walk again and that I would probably lose my left foot. I was dismayed, but my faith held steady. When our children finally rolled me upstairs to see Charles, I just sat there and wept, holding his swollen hand. He appeared to be oblivious, but we talked to him, sang, prayed, and read the Bible. As they rolled me back to my room, I cried, "Oh, Charles! Will I ever hear your dear voice again?" That night as I slept fitfully, I felt the reassurance of my faith in God and His ability to heal and restore sweeping over me.

Following a four-week stay in the hospital, I was finally discharged. Although my doctors told me that I would be in a wheelchair for months and would likely never walk again, I kept talking to the Great Physician and never doubted that He could touch both Charles and me in a glorious way.

It was a great day when Charles emerged from the coma. He was hospitalized for a total of 16 weeks for treatment and therapy. Although he lost the sight in one eye and had restricted use of his right arm, he was gradually able to return to ministry. His doctors thought his progress was amazing.

I also astonished the medical establishment when I got out of my wheelchair and walked with the help of a walker. I was so glad that my left foot had not been amputated. Since that November night we have experienced tremendous physical pain and difficulty getting around. Charles and I have both endured multiple surgeries and great changes in our lives. But our faith has not been shaken. God has sustained us and renewed us at every turn.

I might appear to walk slowly and painfully, but my walk of faith is steady and strong as I lean on the arm of the Great Physician.

MARY THOMPSON AND HER HUSBAND, CHARLES, HAVE SERVED IN MINISTRY FOR MORE THAN 40 YEARS. CHARLES IS SUPERINTENDENT OF THE VIRGINIA DISTRICT OF THE CHURCH OF THE NAZARENE. THEY HAVE THREE CHILDREN AND RESIDE IN RICHMOND, VIRGINIA.

JOYCE WILLIAMS
IT'S TRUE—I WOULDN'T HAVE BELIEVED IT!

$\mathcal{T}$hese years have been incredible beyond my wildest dreams. The promise of Hab. 1:5 has been fulfilled repeatedly as God has blessed my life. Gene and I have traveled extensively in the United States and around the world.

I enjoyed being a pastor's wife for more than five years. The people at Wichita First Church of the Nazarene graciously accepted me. Gene and his late wife, Bettye, had pastored there for more that 19 years before her death, and she was the ultimate pastor's wife.

I was not typical in some ways—like playing the piano. So I wrote a poem about being a pastor's wife, titled "She Can't Even Play the Piano." It's a great compliment to those wonderful people at Wichita First Church, acknowledging the fact that they made room in their hearts for me too.

I've had times of tears as well as great joy. My dear mother died less than a year after Gene and I were married. Gene preached her funeral. My daughter Bethany has been critically ill several times over these years, but God has watched over her. The people in our church prayed for her, and time after time the Lord restored her. During those tough times He enabled me to write my poem "Tears in a Bottle."

When the time came for us to retire, we didn't know what God had in mind for us. But I distinctly remember the day when God made it clear. I had been praying that God would release Gene to retire at just the right point, as I knew it was going to be very hard for him to step aside after 47 years in the pastorate. In his own words, he was "addicted to pastoring." As is often the case, there were some who knew it was time for us to go before we did. So I thanked God that Saturday when He clarified His will for Gene to resign the next day.

The timing sure didn't seem right. Gene was preparing for the annual missions conference at our church. Also, he had been very instrumental in bringing a Franklin Graham Festival to Wichita. But when God made it clear, Gene didn't hesitate. We had discussed possible retirement with our district superintendent on several occasions. So Gene called him and confirmed, "Tomorrow is the day." But I must confess that our faith was stretched to the max!

I wouldn't want to go back through that Sunday morning. It was tough, and Gene was torn to pieces. It was like ripping out his heart to tell his people, "I will no longer be your pastor." But we knew it was God's timing. And immediately doors of opportunity began bursting open.

The next day, Tex Reardon, who had organized the festival, called and asked us to meet with him on Tuesday. As we sat across the table from him, he said, "Now that you won't be pastoring, would both of you consider doing some assignments with the Billy Graham Evangelistic Association?" We prayed through in about five seconds! Our Father is a great compensator. He opened a wonderful door of opportunity far beyond anything we dreamed.

The Lord also prompted both of us about beginning a ministry to pastoral families. Gene had so much to share, and we began to know it was God's plan. One evening as we pulled into our cul-de-sac, Gene said, "Shepherds' Fold Ministries. That's what we'll call it. God wants us to feed the feeders!" And I knew immediately that this was exactly right.

In December Gene went to Minneapolis for training. Because of the generosity of friends, Millard Reed invited us to come to our alma mater, Trevecca Nazarene University, in Nashville for two months each year for four years as pastors in residence.

Our last Sunday at Wichita First Church was January 11, 1998, Gene's 66th birthday. The next day we headed for Alexandria, Louisiana, to work with Franklin Graham's pre-crusade team. Calls came in, and our calendar was filled up with a great variety of experiences. The church was extremely generous and gracious to us in our send-off, so we are able to live comfortably and stay in our new home. We agree that we are blessed beyond expression.

The theme of these years could be "on the road—or in the air—again!" Our experiences have far exceeded our dreams. Speaking in nearly 100 venues in the United States as well as in other countries has been enormously rewarding. Working with the Billy Graham Evangelistic Association in over 20 different assignments continues to be a great blessing. Shepherds' Fold Ministries has expanded beyond our imagination. Our four years at Trevecca were wonderful. And it goes on and on.

With all these wonderful opportunities and challenges, my prayer life has expanded by necessity. Each year the Lord gives a theme to me so I can focus on His agenda when I speak for retreats and other events. In 2000 He told me to emphasize prayer. I have a difficult time concentrating with my type A personality, so I began to really pray about praying! I remembered the prayers I've prayed over the years—never enough—but still a lot. One day I asked the Lord, *Where have all those prayers gone?* In a few minutes He led me to Rev. 5:6-8, which tells us that our prayers are collected in golden bowls in the throne room of the Lamb. Then He gave me the poem "No Prayer Is Ever Wasted."

If we had been designing a blueprint for what we would like to do, we would not have been audacious enough to ask for what God has given to us. And as the promise says, even if He had told us, we wouldn't have believed all He's provided! We are just holding on tight and enjoying the journey—wondering what's around the next bend.

Oh, and by the way, my Prince Charming and I celebrated our 10th wedding anniversary in San Juan, Puerto Rico in August 2002—on the beach.

Thank You, Father, for giving us unshakable faith in even the shakiest times.

JOYCE WILLIAMS

NO PRAYER IS EVER WASTED

My heart was heavy burdened
   As I bowed there by my bed,
Recallng a lifetime of prayers
   And countless tears I'd shed.

I cried out from my heart,
   "Lord, where do my prayers go?
I know You hear them all,
   For the Bible tells me so."

Then my eyes fell on the pages,
   And your Word to me was shown.
Hope swelled within as I read,
   "Your prayers are kept by my throne.

"For NO PRAYER IS EVER WASTED;
   I keep them in bowls made of gold.
They're the very fragrance of heaven;
   Their aroma can never be told.

"That precious pungent perfume
   Is the essence that does pervade
The halls and streets of My city,
   Gathered each time you pray."

My heart was filled with gladness
  At that scene before the throne.
Our Father collects our prayers
  To perfume His heavenly home!

To think that the sacred scent
  Drifting on the heavenly breeze
Flows there from the faithful saints
  Who spend time with Him on their knees.

All the prayers we pray
  Fly straight to that heavenly realm.
They're the aroma in the nostrils of God
  In the throne room of the Lamb!

(Based on Rev. 5:6-8)

BEVERLEY LONDON

MY PRIORITY

I'd never recommend it, but H. B. and I got married when I was 19 and he was 20. We were much too young. H. B. had suffered some reversals in college and needed a change—so we got married.

Thank God for godly influences in our lives. Because of that, we got our lives back on track spiritually. As unlikely as it seemed to both of us, H. B. was called into the ministry. So we headed back to college and then on to seminary in Kansas City. With very little money and with Brad, our newborn son, we had no clue as to what to expect in the uncharted years ahead.

We did everything that we could do to learn everything we could. Finally, in 1962 we moved into our first little parsonage in Whittier, California. In 1963 Bryan, our second son, joined us. There we were—a family of four—with a loving congregation that had great expectations for us. The truth was, though, that many of their expectations were unrealistic.

H. B. came from a long line of clergy families. In fact, he was a fourth-generation pastor. I was from a family of faithful churchgoers, but there was no way I was ready for the demands of living in the fishbowl of a parsonage.

H. B.'s mom was a super pastor's wife, and because of that, she had been his only point of comparison. The truth is that he expected me to be just like her. Believe me—I wasn't!

That was difficult for him. In reality that difference caused both of us a great deal of conflict. He had the notion that our validation as a clergy family would be determined by the level of my activity and involvement in the church. It had been my understanding all along that my primary role was to be a wife and a mother. He was a workaholic shepherd; I was a "nester." He wanted to build a church; I wanted to establish a home. It took us a while to find our stride, and when we did, our life in the pastorate for more than three decades was filled with challenges but with many more blessings.

If I had any advice to give to other pastors' wives, it would be in one simple phrase: Be yourself. And have faith in God's guidance. With the encouragement of your husband, do your best. Find a pace you can keep without exhausting yourself, and regardless of the size of your church, view it as your sanctuary—a place for your family to call home, a place to deepen the roots of your faith.

You may often wonder how your children will remember and reflect on their lives under the microscope. That concerned us. But our two sons are doing great. In fact, both of them are involved in parachurch-type vocations and are happily married. They've blessed us with four beautiful and handsome grandchildren. Our family is a great source of satisfaction and thanksgiving.

What did we do as clergy parents? We loved them, affirmed them, prayed for them, and when it was time, let them go. We didn't raise them as if they were the property of the church but as our precious children. We let them make their own life choices, provided parameters for their guidance, and taught them to respect the church, school, and authority. When they left for college, we prayed a prayer, shed a tear, took a deep breath, and trusted God with our sons and the decisions we had made.

On Mother's Day 2000 I received a letter from Bryan. He

was led to share some of his feelings for me that seemed to turn back the pages of our family's life. In one paragraph of the letter he wrote,

> From your son's point of view, the greatest thing you have done for me is always being there. You were there to take me to Little League games and basketball practice. You even taught me how to drive. We were your priority. Today it's as easy as picking up the phone to find you. The love and advice you have shown us has helped beyond words. I hope these thoughts make your Mother's Day a happy one, because this is one son who is proud to say, "I love you, Mom"!

Needless to say, that brought more than one tear to both of us. We thank God for our kids and the wonderful congregations that loved and nurtured them through their developing years.

Please don't ever give up on your children. Don't ever let them feel that they're playing second fiddle to the congregations you serve. Whatever you do, pray for them every day. Then have faith enough to set them free. God *will* respond to you. That's *His* promise—not mine, but His!

In one of H. B.'s books he used the scripture from 2 Tim. 1:5 to accentuate the value of a mother's influence on the home. Paul wrote, "I have been reminded of your sincere faith, which first lived in your grandmother Lois and your mother Eunice and, I am persuaded, now lives in you also." What a wonderful tribute! Thank God for giving me the wisdom to establish the right priorities. I'm still clipping coupons!

BEVERLEY LONDON IS AN INTERIOR DESIGN CONSULTANT FOR FOCUS ON THE FAMILY. SHE AND HER HUSBAND, H. B., SERVED IN PASTORAL MINISTRY FOR 31 YEARS BEFORE JOINING FOCUS ON THE FAMILY IN 1991. THEY HAVE TWO SONS AND RESIDE IN COLORADO SPRINGS.

OLIVE TAYLOR-PEARCE

AND REMEMBER: JESUS LOVES YOU

I wish I could wipe the memories of January 1999 from my mind. That's when the rebel army invaded Sierre Leone. On January 6 my husband, Modupe, and I gathered with our friends for our regular diocesan prayer meeting. Our dear sister, Rexina Rex-Johnson, shared experiences of her treatment by the soldiers and stories of her escape. She asked us to pray and fast so that the dark cloud of evil that was engulfing our country could be wiped out. After a good and encouraging prayer meeting, we left with the agreement that we should fast and pray for 21 days.

About 3 A.M. the next morning the jangling of our phone interrupted our troubled sleep. A friend who lives on the east side of Freetown was calling to tell us that the rebels had entered our city. Modupe and I began to pray fervently. Just at daybreak we heard the sound of many people moving in our direction. We looked out our window and could see them passing by our house in droves. They were all shapes and sizes—little children, young girls, women with babies on their backs, boys, and men. They passed by to the central prison that was at the end of our road. We began to hear shooting, and it wasn't long before they were streaming back the other direction. The rebel army had broken into the prison and had released the incorrigible inmates. Bullets began to fall on our roof like raindrops. Our world was shaking around us.

For eight days our part of the city was under siege as the government had lost control. The rebels barged into houses and took anything they wanted, including young girls and boys. One day I left the room momentarily. Then the Lord said, *Go back to that room and tell Modupe to get out of that chair.* I ran in there and said, "Leave immediately!" As soon as he got to the door, several bullets penetrated the chair in which he had been sitting.

During the evening of January 12 the rebels came through our streets demanding that everyone come out of their homes waving a white cloth and singing, "We want peace!" They threatened to set our homes on fire if we did not obey their commands. Modupe and the older children who were with us complied, leaving my 95-year-old mother-in-law and a little girl inside with me.

I sat in the den praying. I heard a knock on our back door. Then it was flung open, and Modupe stumbled into the room, followed by two rebel soldiers, a colonel and his sergeant, who had their guns pointed at his back. Modupe cried out, "Darling, we have visitors!"

Without hesitation I replied, "Welcome—come in!" Both of the soldiers had an elastoplast on their right temples. We later discovered that this bandage covered the incision they had made to use cocaine. Our niece was very frightened and ran into the bedroom. That made the soldiers wild, and they pointed their guns at her, ready to pull the trigger. Modupe restrained them, and they calmed down.

Colonel James turned to me and asked, "You are one of those Creole politicians, aren't you?" I said nothing. They saw sodas left over from Christmas and began stuffing them into their pockets. Then they opened our freezer and pointed with

their guns to the items they wanted. Sergeant Sanoh asked if I
had rice, which I did. There was a good quantity of leftover
food in the house since we were fasting. I brought food to
them and set it on the table, pushing aside our Bibles and
hymnbooks. I served them as though we had invited them to
dinner. One wanted ice in his water glass, and the other didn't
want ice. I gave them salt to flavor their food.

As they ate, Modupe kept telling Colonel James that Jesus
loved him. When Colonel James told us that he was in charge
of burning houses, Modupe continued to talk about Jesus'
love. Then Modupe asked if he could pray with them. Colonel
James responded, "You had better pray for yourselves!"

When he finished eating, Colonel James asked, "Could
your God forgive me?"

Modupe replied, "Jesus Christ forgave a thief who had
been condemned to death, and I believe that Jesus Christ will
forgive you if you're sincere. You see, Jesus loves you! I will
pray and ask God to forgive you if you will pray the prayer
with me."

When Modupe asked Colonel James if there was anything
else he would like to pray for, his answer amused me. He said,
"Ask Him to give me a long life and good health." I realized
how much those who kill and destroy fear death for themselves.

Modupe said, "We should kneel down to pray, and both of
them did that—without any hesitation. Modupe prayed a
lengthy prayer. (I later told him it was much too long!) When
he finished praying, they got up to leave, and Modupe walked
them to the door like honored guests. Then he said, "I would
like to invite you to come and join us for our Bible study. We
meet every Monday at 5 P.M." Frankly, I was glad they were
leaving and thought that inviting them to come back was a
little much! Wasn't this stretching God's grace too far?

Altogether, they were in our house for 30 to 45 minutes,

through the entire time God gave me a calmness that could come only from Him. It was as though the Spirit of God had covered and insulated me from fear of the enemy. We could have been blown to pieces at any moment. Some professor friends of ours were murdered during that time in a similar situation. The rebels had their guns, grenades, and were high on cocaine.

Modupe always says, "How you respond to a crisis is determined by how you're living before the crisis comes." Since our entire life was a faith-based walk, when faced with disaster, our confidence in God's deliverance held us steady.

I remember watching Modupe stand at the door to see the soldiers off as though they were friends. He called out one more time, "And remember—Jesus loves you!"

Our faith in that truth is what holds us steady in shaky times.

OLIVE TAYLOR-PEARCE IS A SPEAKER, WRITER, AND PRAYER WARRIOR. SHE AND HER HUSBAND, MODUPE, FOUNDED AND DIRECT THE DIAKONIA INTERDENOMINATIONAL SERVICES FOR COUNSELING, EVANGELISM, AND TRAINING. THEY RESIDE IN FREETOWN, SIERRA LEONE, WEST AFRICA.

VICKI TIAHRT

SEPTEMBER 11, 2001, IN WASHINGTON, D.C.

t was a perfect fall morning—crisp and cool, beautiful and bright. Everything looked wonderful, but it has been described as the day that changed the world forever. I was at home in Fairfax, Virginia, just outside of the beltway of Washington, D.C. My husband, Todd, had left for his office at the Capitol, and our sons, John and Luke, had left for school. Our daughter, Jessica, was readying herself for her college classes.

The peace of that morning was broken by the shrill ring of the telephone. Todd was on the line. "Turn on the TV, Vicki. A plane has flown into the World Trade Center". His voice was urgent, tense, and persistent. He was listening to the car radio and heard of the first plane's crash into the south tower. He hung up, driving into heavy traffic.

I turned on the television set and watched the towering inferno along with the rest of the world. It was unfathomable. There was no way to understand what was happening. The news anchors were struggling, giving differing eyewitness accounts. Some reported a small plane, an accident. Others were reporting a passenger jet. And then, as I watched, another plane flew into the other tower. It was obvious to everyone watching that this was not an accident. America was under attack!

I was glued to the television, watching the chaos as the

towers burned and then collapsed, and my heart was sickened and heavy. Then a report came that there were other planes off track. I gasped as I waited. Then it happened. A tremendous crash shook the patio door. Washington had been hit.

My heart was pounding, my mouth dry as I quickly tried to dial Todd on his cell phone. There was no dial tone. I went to the computer—no connection. I tried the fax machine—no tone. Trying to calculate where he would be on his commute to the Capitol, I was sure he was in harm's way.

The report came over the air that the Pentagon had been hit by a plane. In the horror of that moment, I just wanted to be sure my husband and my children were safe. Todd often drives north on I-395, which goes right by the Pentagon. I tried to call again and was able to get through to his Congressional office. The staff there told me they were all right and that Todd was on the line with them. He had been just south of the Pentagon when the plane hit. He saw the first cloud and then the tremendous plume of black smoke. He knew it was an airplane.

The news in D.C. was crazy on September 11. False bomb reports were widespread. Then word came that a plane had crashed in Pennsylvania. The Capitol and White House were evacuated as potential targets. Unlike Pearl Harbor, no one knew who this enemy was. Along with the rest of the world, life in the nation's capital has changed forever.

To be totally honest, my initial inclination was to leave the area, pack up our sons, and head for Kansas's peaceful prairies. But how could I leave Todd and Jessica? There just was no way I could head for safety with only half of our family. I prayed and shared with friends and family.

Congressional families debated the best course of action. Some left Washington. A young mother said, "I'll be just like Molly Pitcher and stay in this fight," as she smiled with fierce determination. Another friend, whose husband has been assigned to dangerous areas with the State Department, told me how to prepare for a speedy departure, packing a change of clothes for everyone, storing water, food, and survival gear in the car trunk, and keeping the gas tank full.

We have all reconsidered our activities. Memorial services, the State of Union address, any large gathering of officials is a potential target for terrorism. Some families choose to stay away completely, while some parents determine that only one will attend so that if the worst happens, the children will have one surviving parent.

So how do we live in the face of terror? And particularly, how do we who follow Christ live without fear when we're so despised and targeted for destruction as infidels?

"God has not given us a spirit of fear, but of power and of love and of a sound mind" (2 Tim. 1:7, NKJV). Paul's writing is particularly poignant today. As I struggled with issues of safety following September 11, I went back to these words. This is a scripture I had learned in childhood but had never studied in the whole. I read through Paul's letters to Timothy, focusing on that passage. With booming authority, firmly based on lived experience, Paul's words comfort and compel us today.

We have chosen to stay in Fairfax—to stay together, to live the life we believe God has for us here in this hot spot—not because we're strong or brave or ignorant of the danger. But because God is in full control, and "God has not given us a spirit of fear, but of power and of love and of a sound mind."

VICKI TIAHRT HELPED ESTABLISH A CONGRESSIONAL PRAYER GROUP CALLED WIVES. SHE AND HER HUSBAND, TODD, WHO HAS SERVED IN THE UNITED STATES HOUSE OF REPRESENTATIVES FOR EIGHT YEARS, HAVE THREE CHILDREN. THEY RESIDE IN FAIRFAX, VIRGINIA.

PATSY CLAIRMONT

AN ACT OF FAITH

*I*t takes an act of faith to get onto an airplane today! None of us will ever forget where we were on September 11, 2001, when "911" became more than an emergency phone number. Our hearts will always beat a little quicker when we walk down that caterpillar tube that's suctioned to the plane. And every time anyone gets up to go to the bathroom, we take a second look just in case.

Since I ride planes all of the time as I run back and forth across this country, I've had to adjust to all the delays, lost luggage, and pretzel pieces in my shoes. A cup of ice in my lap is not a heartwarming experience. These and other minor inconveniences don't get the attention they used to. Now everybody is so glad to arrive at his or her destination that griping is almost a thing of the past.

One thing I've noticed: it sure is easier to share my faith these days. Especially the first weeks and months after the attacks, almost everybody held captive in the seat next to me was willing to talk about God. It has been gratifying to see so many people returning to the faith of their youth.

But the truth is, living a life based on faith has always been available. The good news is that we don't have to wait for a tragedy or an emergency to tap into God's resources. As a matter of fact, the best plan is to make trusting the Lord a way of life even when things are normal (if they ever are!).

Then, even when our world starts shaking and the ground is quaking, our faith will hold us steady.

So I'm still climbing on planes and shaking pretzel pieces from my shoes. And I'm more excited than ever about seeing who my next captive seatmate might be. For, you see, in these uncertain times I don't want to just keep the faith—I want to be a faith spreader!

PATSY CLAIRMONT IS A WELL-KNOWN AUTHOR OF NUMEROUS BEST-SELLING BOOKS. SHE IS IN GREAT DEMAND AS A SPEAKER AND TRAVELS REGULARLY WITH WOMEN OF FAITH CONFERENCES, HAVING SPOKEN TO MORE THAN 1 MILLION WOMEN IN RECENT YEARS. SHE AND HER HUSBAND, LES, HAVE TWO SONS AND RESIDE IN BRIGHTON, MICHIGAN.

JOYCE WILLIAMS

UNSHAKABLE FAITH FOR SHAKY TIMES

In those years of shaky faith
  My heart was enslaved by fear,
Until I came to the end of myself
  When God himself drew near.

Battered, bruised, and broken,
  With a dagger piercing my soul,
I cried out, "I can't do this!
  Please come and make me whole!"

Then He answered, "Someday you'll forget your troubles,
  And no one will make you afraid.
You'll take your rest in safety
  And have peace in the years just ahead.

"You see, the battle's not yours, my child.
  The words I tell you are true.
I've been waiting all these years
  To fight all your battles for you."

My fears vanished like a vapor;
  And I was afraid no more,
For my soul had found a sweet rest
  In the harbor of faith's peaceful shore.

Freedom is found in surrender
 As we come to the end of ourselves.
Holding tight to His unfailing love
 While letting go of everything else.

And in the darkest nights—God's promises
 Shine like the stars high above
As they weave a tapestry of faith
 That covers us with His great love.

So when our world shakes all around us
 As we plod through the quicksands of life,
If we hold tight to our faith in our Father,
 He'll guide us through all of the strife.

With a faith that's firm and true,
 Built on His rock and not sand.
Shaky times on the pathway of life
 Are held steady in our Father's hands.

Be still, and know that I am God.
—Ps. 46:10